California State & Local Government in Crisis

2nd Edition

Walt Huber

Glendale College

Educational Textbook Company
P.O. Box 3597
Covina, California 91722
(818) 3397733

Includes Index

Library of Congress Cataloging in Publication Data

Huber, Walter Roy
California State & Local Government in Crisis

ISBN #0-916772-53-5

320.9794

1. California Politics and Government
2. Political Participation

I. Huber, Walter R., 1941 II. Title.

Printed in California, U.S.A.

Preface

When asked about California's political problems, the professors who take part in our surveys overwhelmingly state that most of California's big problems are created or related to our huge population growth. The word "crisis" keeps surfacing time and time again. These contributing professors are the guiding force behind our editorial policy. We constantly survey these professors in order to continually improve our reputation as the most up-to-date and comprehensive textbook on California politics. To these professors we owe a special thanks and acknowledge them and their college in the front of this book.

Editorials or current topics of discussion are found in rectangular boxes. We do express our personal opinions, but only in the Editorial boxes.

The extensive index at the back of the book is especially designed to be student friendly. Also, you will enjoy the way that important vocabulary words are typeset in **BOLDFACE** type throughout the textbook and how easy to follow definitions are set in *script.* They cover any term that a first time college student would need in a California state and local government course.

I want to express my appreciation to the following people whose contributions were invaluable to me in the writing of this book Professor Marilyn Loufek of Long Beach City College, Valerie Hunt, Ric Williams and William Parker of Glendale College, Dr. Cecilia Batnag-Palacal of Chaffey College, Lance Widman of El Camino College, Dr. Owen Newcomer of Rio Hondo College, Tony Bernhard of University of California, Davis and Professor Reece of Cerritos College.

Special thanks also to Philip Dockter, art director; Rick Lee, executive editor; Tim Doyle, editor; Linn Baker for revision advice and our Sacramento connection, Joseph Dooling.

I thank Carol Hamilton who manages our office and Professor Marcy Morris from Citrus College. But most of all, I thank our surveyed professors who set the standards for this two year effort to create a book especially designed for freshmen and sophomores. I proudly acknowledge each for their valuable input.

Walt Huber

Acknowledgments

Joseph Krinsky
William L. Uttenweiler
Allan Hancock College

Bruce Rogers
Peter Howse
American River College

Art R. Aurand
Donald R. Ranish
Antelope Valley College

Gregory L. Goodwin
James B. Inskeep
Bakersfield College

Richard Reeb Jr.
Barstow College

Steven A. Holmes
Butte College

Gary Carlson
C. Bailey
Cabrillo College

Theodore Reller
Canada College

Thomas Sevener
Cerritos College

Chester D. Rhoan
Chabot College

Robert Melsh
Michael Viera
Robin Gass
Chaffey College

Neil Lucas
College of Alameda

Joanne Roney Carpenter
Donald F. Cate
College of San Mateo

Russell Richardson
College of the Canyons

Gary Wiedle
College of the Desert

Daniel Faulk
Glenn Stockwell
College of the Redwoods

W. Peterson, Ph.D.
College of the Sequoias

Jim Ray
College of the Siskiyous

Albert Rose
Prof. Rodriguez
Compton College

Rocco C. Chavez
Ted Radke
Contra Costa College

Frank Kashuk
Cuesta College

Robert Holden
Cuyamaca College

Denese Wecker
Carol Marquis Alen
Cypress College

James Hanley
De Anza College

V. W. Woolbright
Diablo Valley College

Joel Busch
East Los Angeles College

Daniel Gregory, Ph.D.
L. Widman
El Camino College

Alfred M. Alexander
Evergreen Valley College

Rolland C. Rogers
Foothill College

Robert Arroyo
Richard Bartels
Fresno City College

Abdulla Sindi, Ph.D.
Fullerton College

Frank Fletcher
Gavilan College

Julie Flake
James C. Gilchrist
Drake Hawkins
William Parker
Mark Weaver
Valerie Hunt
Glendale College

Gregory Ghica
Thomas A. Chambers
Golden West College

Adrienne Karel Leffler
Grossmont College

Thomas C. Bilello
Irvine Valley College

Marilin Fuller-Newquest
William Hutton
Drew Featherston
Marilyn J. Loufek
Sue Nelson
John D. Chamberlain
Long Beach City College

Philip J. Schlessinger
Doyle Bates
Ronald Pelton
Los Angeles City College

William Loiterman
Los Angeles Harbor College

Joseph L. DeTorres
Los Mendanos College

Kerman Maddox
L. A. Southwest College

Charles Weymann
Richard Kazie
Lawrence C. Jorgensen
Los Angeles Valley College

Michael Levine
Merced College

Sarbjit Johal, Ph.D.
Merritt College

Acknowledgments

Randy Siefkin
Modesto College

Henry Pacheco
L. Shipman
Maxine Sparks-Mackey
Mt. San Antonio College

Paul Bonaccorsi
Alan Kirshner
Howard A. Dewitt
Ohlone College

John Buckley
Thomas Wert
Orange Coast College

M. Newbrough
Warren Hawley
Palomar College

Kevin Eoff
Palo Verde College

G. R. Patterson
Porterville College

David Hartman
Rancho Santiago College

Owen Newcomer, Ph.D.
Henry H. Goldman
Ted Snyder
Rio Hondo College

William L. Swinehart
Kristina Kauffman Cline
Riverside Comm. College

W. Patrick Kirklin
Terrence W. Leveille
Sacramento City College

Tom Moody
Saddleback College

Vincent B. Lynch
San Francisco City College

Donald H. Estes
Lisa Matt
Myles L. Clowers
Joel James Snyder
San Diego City College

Carl Luna
Sam H. Farahani, Ph.D.
Ken Payne
Joe Mckenzie
Thomas B. Mack, Jr., Ph.D.
San Diego Mesa College

Earnest Glannecchini
Michael McGuire
San Joaquin Delta College

Jan Henry Groenen
San Jose City College

D. Lawyer
John Kay
Santa Barbara City College

Faisal H. Tbeileh
Santa Monica College

John Overn
W. R. Massey
Gus P'manolis
Santa Rosa College

Larry Wight
Sierra College

Jean Baxter
B. Thurston
Richard Gelm
Solano College

Richard M. Ybarra
Alma Aguilar
Southwestern College

Kent Quinn
Ventura College

Norine E. Oliver
Raymond E. Smith
West Hills College

Jack D. Ruebensaal
Mark Weaver
West Los Angeles College

Adam Stone
West Valley College

David Rubiales
Yuba College

Table of Contents

CHAPTER 1 — *California In Crisis*

CHAPTER 2 — *Early History and The Federal Government*

CHAPTER 3 — *Voters, Primaries and General Elections*

CHAPTER 4 — *Direct Democracy*

CHAPTER 5 — *Interest Groups, Political Parties And Campaigns*

CHAPTER 6 — *The Executive Branch*

CHAPTER 7 — *The California Legislature: Our Lawmakers*

CHAPTER 8 — *Our Judicial System*

CHAPTER 9 — *Cities and Counties At The Crossroads*

CHAPTER 10 — *Our State Budget Crisis*

CHAPTER 1 California In Crisis

CALIFORNIA IS IN A CRISIS!

California, the golden state for so many decades, is starting to realize that times have changed. California is in a crisis. We must face the fact that our constantly growing population has finally created big problems that require immediate attention. Our highways are congested, schools are overcrowded, housing costs have soared, health care and welfare for our poor is grossly inadequate, criminals are pouring into our jails and the quality of our air and water is declining.

The sad fact is—there are no simple answers anymore. We can't just increase our already high state taxes or we will force the very people who pay the most taxes to leave the state.

California's Growth Problem

ABOUT GROWTH

FACT: California has 12% of the nation's population.

"The critical challenge facing California is to accommodate the growth that is projected to occur. If we do not, the problems that we currently face—traffic congestion, air and water pollution, inadequate housing, overcrowded jails, and insufficient public facilities—will increase dramatically." **Pete Wilson**

FACT: There are 1,650 new Californians every 24 hours, most are immigrants or children of immigrants.

The fact is California's population is growing rapidly because of our easily accessible borders, economic opportunities, unmatched by other states or nations, and because recent immigrants tend to have relatively high birth rates.

The "golden state" should really be called the "growth state." By the year 2000, there will be another 6 million people—we will have grown from 30 million people to 36 million.

The 1990 Census indicates that one of nine U.S. residents lives in California. Over the last decade, one-fourth of the U.S. population growth occurred in California.

JOBS DRAW PEOPLE TO CALIFORNIA

FACT: The state's population keeps growing because the number of jobs in California keeps growing.

Jobs are the primary factor that encourage people to migrate here. People come for these jobs despite high housing prices, congested highways and environmental problems.

PROBLEMS CREATED BY THE RECESSION OF 1990

California, along with the rest of the nation, went into a recession in 1990. California did not come out of it until after 1993. While a recession is considered a normal part of any business cycle, this recession is deeper and likely to last longer because it coincides with the restructuring of a major California industry—defense. The nation, through base closures, has been able to cut defense spending, a so-called "peace dividend" that resulted from the ending of the Cold War. The defense industry's work in California has been slowing down for some time but the effects of the Soviet Union break-up have accelerated the down-sizing of defense.

The unemployment caused by this action will increase the number of skilled defense workers who may be out of a job for some years to come in California. This is referred to as

California's Ethnic Diversity

Racial and ethnic population in California, according to 1990 Census.

CALIFORNIA

CENSUS '90

ASIANS	
Filipino	731,685
Chinese	704,850
Japanese	312,898
Vietnamese	280,223
Korean	259,941
Indian	159,973
Laotian, Cambodian, Thai	158,312
Hmong	46,892
All others	38,831
PACIFIC ISLANDERS	
Hawaiian	34,447
Samoan	31,917
Guamanian	25,059
Tongan	7,919
HISPANICS	
Mexican	6,118,996
Puerto Rican	126,417
Cuban	71,977
All Others Combined (census did not break others down)	1,370,548

ETHNIC BREAKDOWN

WHITE (NON-HISPANIC) - 57.2%	17 million
BLACK, AFRO-AMERICAN - 7%	2.1 million
HISPANIC - 25.8%	7.7 million
ASIAN and Other -9.9%	2.98 million
CALIFORNIA (Rounded)	***29.8 million***

structural unemployment. Unemployment from a recession is temporary but structural unemployment is permanent. ***STRUCTURAL UNEMPLOYMENT*** *is a permanent change in employment patterns for a given industry that has long lasting effects and creates long-term unemployment in that industry.*

CALIFORNIA'S GROWING ETHNIC DIVERSITY

FACT: 40% of all Californians are Asian, Black or Hispanic.

About one-half of our growth in the last decade was due to immigration from other countries. The other half was due to births exceeding deaths. Overall, about 75% of the growth in the last decade occurred among ethnic minorities, primarily Hispanics, Blacks and Asians. Of the 30 million people in California, about 40%, or 12.5 million, are Hispanics, Asians and Blacks. This minority share should rise to almost 50% by the year 2000.

Asians are the fastest growing group in California. They have increased 125% from 1980 to 1990, for a total of 3 1/2 million in California. Over 9.9% of all Californians are of Asian ancestry. This percentage will also increase year-after-year.

Of course, when we say "Asian," we are combining a large number of cultures. The Chinese, our first Asian immigrants, were brought here in the 1860's as a cheap labor pool to build our railroads. But since that time, there has been a large influx of Japanese, Korean and people from the Vietnam region.

In 1990, 40% of all Californians were non-white. As mentioned previously, this figure will grow to over 50% by the year 2000.

Ethnic mix and race will continue to vary from city-to-city. This will be a greater challenge to California than it has been in the past.

Hispanics and Asians generally tend to have larger families than Blacks while Whites have the fewest number of children. According to the 1990 census, Hispanics, Blacks and Asians accounted for 90% of the total increase in the number of children born between 1980 and 1990.

Proposition 187

Proposition 187 was an anti-illegal immigration measure, the most explosive provisions of which bar illegal immigrants from the state's schools and require educators to check on the citizenship status of all students. The measure prohibits the delivery of public services, except emergency medical care, to illegal immigrants.

It sparked numerous protests and demonstrations. A demonstration against the proposition in East Los Angeles drew 70,000. Demonstrators carried placards and waved Mexican flags. In Van Nuys and Chatsworth, thousands of impassioned teenagers marched in protest.

Pete Wilson, a possible 1996 presidential candidate, insisted that the only way California could get the federal government to pay for services to illegal immigrants was to pass Proposition 187. President Clinton, along with Republicans William Bennett and Jack Kemp, came out against the proposition. Proposition 187 seems to have defined an issue that will carry through to the presidential election of 1996.

The Mexican government, known for their neutrality, actively worked with human rights groups and other organizations to bring down the proposition.

Although this proposition passed, it has raised constitutional issues that will surely find a resolution in the U.S. Supreme Court.

Wilson sues U.S. Over Immigrants. Before the passage of Proposition 187, Governor Wilson filed a total of three lawsuits to reimburse California for the cost of providing emergency health care, jail cells and education to illegal immigrants. Annually, 300,000 illegal immigrants receive emergency health care, 18,000 are jailed, and 300,000 attend public school.

It costs California $1.28 billion annually to pay for the education of illegal immigrant children. California and six other states (Florida, Texas, New York, Illinois, Arizona and New Jersey) spend more money on federally mandated (but not funded) programs. Wilson has estimated that illegal immigrants cost the state $3.44 billion annually but pay only $739 million in taxes. **The average illegal immigrant household receives $7,760 in government services each year.**

CALIFORNIA WILL GROW 18% THIS DECADE

FACT: California's population will grow by almost 18% during this decade, while the U.S. population is expected to grow by less than 8%.

Because it is virtually impossible to slow population growth in the state, California's biggest challenge will be how to make room for its daily increase of 1,650 people.

Facing California's Problems

K-12 EDUCATION IS SUFFERING

FACT: California must build 13 new classrooms each day to keep up with the growing number of students.

Kindergarten through 12th grade education has suffered because of California's continuing growth. There are so many students that education is the single largest expense for our state and county governments. As our schools suffer and need more money, voters keep trimming education expenditures because they represent the largest single budget item.

The crush of school age children accelerated greatly in the 1980's. There is no slowdown in sight, as the number of school age children in California should increase by another 1.7 million in the next 10 years. This type of growth will aggravate the already existing problem of demand for classrooms, textbooks, and teachers.

HIGHER EDUCATION IS EXCELLENT

In California, we hear a lot about our K-12 schools struggling for more money, increased space, better high school graduation rates and achievement test scores, but this certainly does not apply to California's colleges.

California colleges are not only the envy of the United States but also the rest of the world, which sends its sons and daughters to study here.

There are over 100 community colleges in California with enrollment of well over a million students. This constitutes about 20% of America's community colleges. Our California State University and University of California systems are highly ranked and still relatively inexpensive to residents of our state. Even with recently increased tuition, higher education is a bargain in California.

California's Most Precious Resource ...Water

1. Continuous water shortages
2. Ground water pollution
3. Environmental concern in Mono basin
4. Arizona is taking more Colorado River water
5. Erratic Weather patterns (drought/flood).

Water wars in the past have pitted:

Northern California vs. Southern California
San Diego vs. Los Angeles
Consumer vs. Agriculture

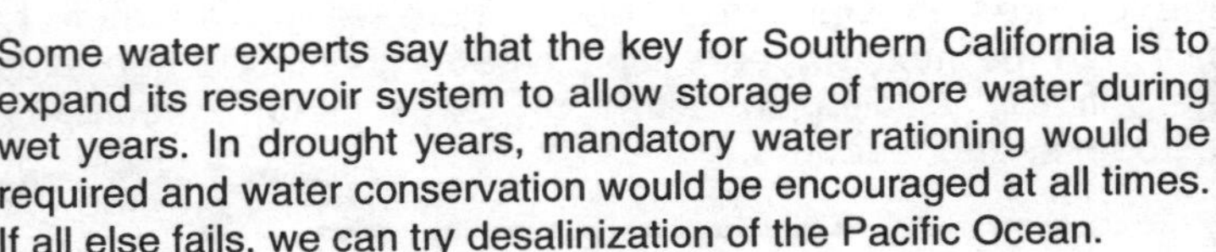

Some water experts say that the key for Southern California is to expand its reservoir system to allow storage of more water during wet years. In drought years, mandatory water rationing would be required and water conservation would be encouraged at all times. If all else fails, we can try desalinization of the Pacific Ocean.

Unlike most other countries that require excellence in K-12 grades, we demand excellence in college work and create opportunities for anyone who wants to finish college. Our downfall is that many students slip through the cracks in the K-12 grades and are not prepared to go on to college. At this time, our system does not provide good vocational alternatives for such students.

BETTER TRANSPORTATION IS NEEDED

FACT: Each day there are 1,000 more cars on our roads.

Until California voters, in 1990, agreed to double their gasoline taxes for transportation, there seemed to be no public interest, for decades, in lowering the freeway travel time. In addition, voters have approved two propositions that will require the issuance of billions of dollars in bonds just to improve and earthquake-proof our crumbling transportation system. This legislation passed as a direct result of the October 17, 1989, Bay Area earthquake. Local voters in 18 counties have approved ballot measures to increase the local sales tax by 0.25% for highway and transit projects. This is one area where California is stepping forward to become a better state by accepting the challenge of improving its crowded roads.

EVEN OUR PRISONS ARE OVERCROWDED

FACT: California has over 100,000 convicts in its prisons. The inmate population grows by 10,000 per year.

By the year 2000, there will be over 200,000 Californians in prison. This will again leave the state's prison system dangerously overcrowded, with no end in sight. The increasing cost and overcrowding renews the old debate about what is the best way to deal with crime and punishment in this state. The "Three Strikes" legislation will cost millions in additional costs for housing and new prisons. Reformers say there must be a better and cheaper way, while at the same time hard-liners feel that we are not strict enough. The cost of keeping a prisoner incarcerated for a year is $20,000. Hard-liners argue, though, that the cost to society would be far greater if criminals were left out on the streets.

AIR QUALITY

Smog, the long-time air problem of Los Angeles, has spread over a large portion of Southern California. With 1,000 more cars on the road each day due to California's increasing population, it is no wonder that the southern part of the state has serious air quality problems. The cherished car is causing most of these problems. As a result, the Air Quality Management District (AQMD) has required organizations with over 100 employees to regulate hours and encourage car pooling.

WASTE MANAGEMENT AND LANDFILLS

Landfill sites in California are filling up fast. As local landfill sites reach their limits, more distant and costly sites must be opened even further from major cities. Recycling can reduce our trash and conserve our resources.

The waste management problem will reach a crisis stage in about a decade when most of Southern California's urban dumps will be filled. That is when trash hauling by train will likely be the most common way of disposal. Cities today pay between $11 and $33 a ton to get rid of their trash. But higher transportation costs, as well as tougher landfill requirements, will soon double this expense. It looks like $50 a ton to dispose of trash will soon seem like a bargain.

HOUSING PROBLEM (CALIFORNIA'S HIGH COST)

The price of real estate in California is resuming its rise after the recession of 1990-1993. This is great for the people who own property, but what about the new buyers? How can they afford to buy a home?

FACT: We must build 550 apartment units, condos or homes each day somewhere in California to keep up with the projected population growth.

With so many new people arriving or being born each day in California, it is no wonder that real estate prices remain high.

The secret of owning a house, "the American Dream," is to start off small. Starter properties are usually found in outer suburbs, are smaller condos or are in lower income areas. When you sell your home, no income taxes are paid on the money you make as long as you buy a more expensive residence within two years.

In the 1990's, the fastest growing population centers will be the Los Angeles area, including Palmdale, Riverside and San Bernardino, which will add more than 2 million people, with the Bay Area and Sacramento adding about 1 million. This accounts for about 60% of the state's new growth.

Facing California's Challenges

It may seem strange to talk at length about California's problems because the state's economy had performed well until the 1990-1993 recession. But California's population growth and growing ethnic diversity are forcing voters increasingly to make urgent and sometimes painful political decisions to ease these growing pains. Politicians will be busy during the rest of the 1990's handling all the challenges that will result from California's continuing population growth.

THE POPULATION GROWTH CHALLENGE

Handling California's growing population and the problems it creates is the number one challenge. There must be a change in the state's priorities, including tax structure and spending options, to deal with the massive population growth that will continue for at least two decades. The real challenge is not how to stop growth but to find ways to slow growth down.

How our state responds to these problems is the major challenge facing California. California politics, like all politics, is the process of arriving at a consensus on how the state is to be governed. In a democracy, our elected officials decide what our laws should be and how the laws are written.

THE PRODUCTIVITY CHALLENGE

Increasing productivity is the key to raising our standard of living. ***PRODUCTIVITY** is the ability to produce an amount of goods and services per working hour.* In our new global economy, the country, state, firm or individual that is more productive will be the one that moves ahead. The concept is simple: accomplish more during the hours you work. Improved management skills will enable us to produce more each hour. It is not necessary to work harder but to work smarter.

If our federal and state governments would encourage (1) more money to be invested in new equipment and state-of-the-art technology and (2) better education for our students and workers, our economy would be more productive! This is how to retain economic power. Productivity was high during the 1950's and 1960's and was considered the smart way to do business. But in the 1970's and 1980's, the growth in productivity began slowing down. Productivity in the 1990's will be the major factor in determining whether our real income and our buying power rise.

THE CULTURAL DIVERSITY CHALLENGE

California's incredible ethnic diversity will pose one of our biggest challenges as we enter the next century. If you look at the census breakdown, you can see the wide-range of cultures represented in the state. Each group has special needs and concerns. With so many different races and cultures living together, how can everyone participate fully and enjoy the benefits of our society without sacrificing their unique cultural integrity? The old "melting pot" idea of assimilation is out. The California of the 21st century will celebrate diversity while it struggles to bring people together in cooperation. The political challenge is for the government to provide services for each diverse group and, at the same time, not raise taxes beyond what is already one of the highest levels in the country.

THE CALIFORNIA BUSINESS CHALLENGE

California businesses are among the most regulated and taxed in the nation. If a business feels that it can make larger profits in the long-run by moving out of state, it will do so. California businesses should be encouraged to stay here, and the perception that California is anti-business must be reversed. When a company moves out of state, jobs are lost and its employees suffer until they find new employment. The tax money once paid by the company that leaves is also lost and if enough companies, or an entire industry, leave the economy will feel the pinch.

If California were a country, it would have the ... 7 th largest economy in the world!

1. U.S. — $5,461 BILLION
2. JAPAN — $2,115 BILLION
3. GERMANY — $1,157 BILLION
4. FRANCE — $874 BILLION
5. BRITAIN — $858 BILLION
6. ITALY — $845 BILLION

7. CALIFORNIA — $600 - $700 BILLION

8. CANADA — $17 BILLION
9. CHINA — $427 (1989) BILLION

"California is Really Big"

(Time November 18, 1991)

California's Growing Economy

FACT: California handles over 20% of all U.S. trade.

Trade is clearly the driving industry in California. Between exports and imports, California has boosted jobs in air transportation, wholesale trades and port facilities. It has also increased such service industries as computer software, entertainment, tourism and professional services. ***EXPORTS** are manufactured goods, agricultural produce, minerals and other items produced in the United States but purchased by other countries. **IMPORTS** are the goods from other countries that Americans purchase.* Names like Mitsubishi, Nissan, Toyota and Hyundai are just a few examples of foreign auto makers whose products are familiar to us all.

CALIFORNIA: A WORLD CLASS ECONOMIC POWER

FACT: California is a world class economic power and ranks 7th in the world.

California is not only a world class economic power but it maintains stability because it is economically diverse. ***ECONOMIC DIVERSITY** means that many economic activities are balanced so that no one industry dominates to the extent that, if eliminated, it would cause problems.* Put another way, all our business and economic eggs are not in one basket. Economic power is measured by gross domestic product. ***GROSS DOMESTIC PRODUCT (GDP)** is the sum of all products and services produced by a country, for personal, governmental and investment purposes, in a given year.*

Overall, about 75% of the population growth in the last decade occurred among ethnic minorities. Asians are the fastest-growing ethnic group in California, increasing 125% in the last decade to make up nearly 10% of the population. Blacks and whites have a more static birth-rate, with Blacks comprising 7% of the state population. Whites make up the largest single group with 57.2%. Hispanics make up 25.8% and have the most children. In 1990, about 40% of our population was "non-white." This number should exceed 50% by the year 2000.

Jobs are still hard to come by as California recovers from an economic recession. The end of the "Cold War" makes matters worse as the U.S. defense industry, much of which is centered in California, is being radically scaled back.

Public education is the state's single largest budget item. No matter how much money we spend we can't seem to keep pace with the growing number of students. We need 13 new classrooms every day to accommodate all the new students.

Every day in California there are another 1,000 automobiles on the roads. New roads and freeways must be built and the present system must be maintained and earthquake-proofed.

Our prisons are also terribly over-crowded. We currently have over a 100,000 people in our prison system. That number will double in ten years. Trash disposal is also reaching a crisis point. Our landfills are filling up quickly. Because water is a precious commodity in California, we have had to buy up water rights elsewhere and build an expensive system of aqueducts to keep our thirsty Southland supplied. Conservation, recycling and desalinization are all being attempted. Needless to say, these solutions will cost money.

One answer to this crisis is a renewed focus on productivity. By investing more in education and new technologies and lifting unnecessary regulations and excessive taxes, we can make California a more viable place for companies to do business. If California were a nation, it would have the seventh largest economy on earth. We are America's gateway to the huge manufacturing centers of the Pacific Rim and Mexico. Trade will be essential to our future. The challenge is to improve the business climate without damaging the quality of life our citizens have come to expect. If we encourage progressive companies to make California their home, the crisis of today could become the economic triumph of tomorrow.

1. What brings so many people to California?

2. What effects does cultural diversity have on California?

3. Are California's problems too overwhelming or do you think we can overcome them? How?

4. How can we reduce overcrowding in the prison system?

5. How can California attract and keep businesses?

THE GREAT SEAL OF THE STATE OF
CALIFORNIA

CHAPTER 2 Early History & The Federal Government

Early California History

CALIFORNIA INDIANS

Native Americans numbered about 150,000 before the Europeans started coming in large numbers to California. The moderate climate and abundant food supply sustained the 135 loosely organized tribes. At one time one/eighth of all American Indians lived in California. California Indians as a whole were friendly and mild-mannered compared to many of the other Indian tribes of the Eastern United States.

The white man greatly contributed to the decline of the Indian population through the introduction of diseases (small pox, malaria, venereal disease), bogus Indian wars, and the destruction of their food supplies. By 1900 there were only about 16,000 Indians remaining in California.

Chapter 2

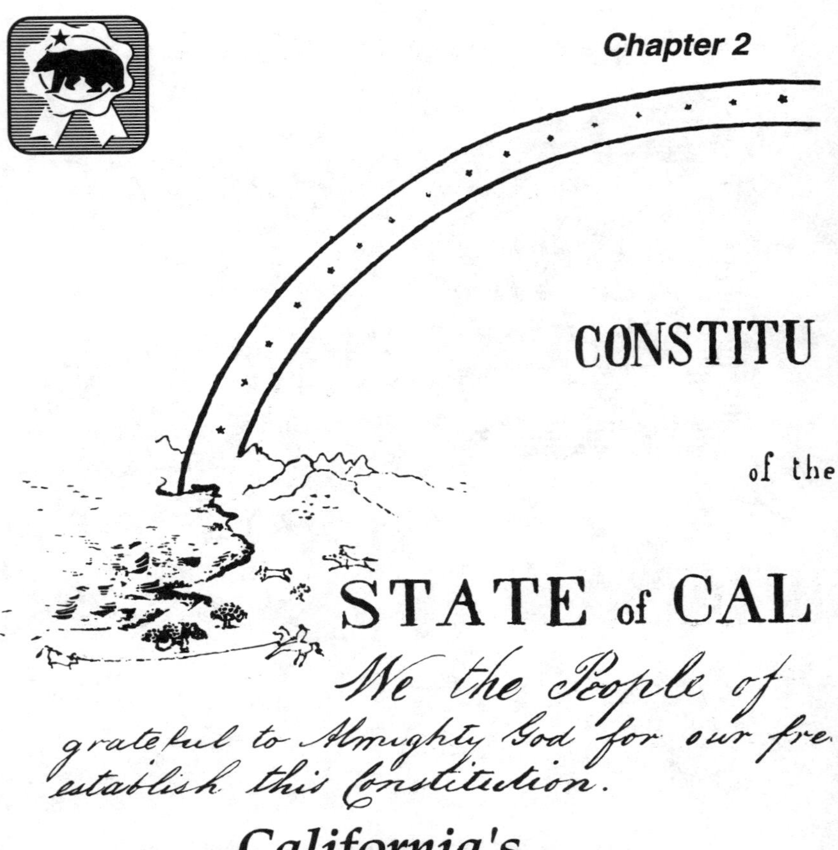

California's Political/Historical Timeline

SUMMARY OF IMPORTANT HISTORICAL DATES

California's Political/Historical Timeline

1500 -- Native Indians who first inhabited the land once numbered 150,000 before the white man introduced his diseases and indifference.

1542 -- Juan Rodriguez Cabrillo discovered San Diego--the first European to set foot in California, only 50 years after Columbus discovered American.

1769 -- Father Junipero Serra began establishing the first of 21 Missions from San Diego to Sonoma--each a one day horseback ride apart.

1821 -- Mexico won its independence from Spain in 1821.

1827 -- Jedediah Smith, the first American to cross the Sierra Mountains, to arrive in California.

1848 -- Gold was discovered by James Marshall near Sacramento at Sutter's sawmill. "Eureka"
(I have found it) -- the gold rush was on.

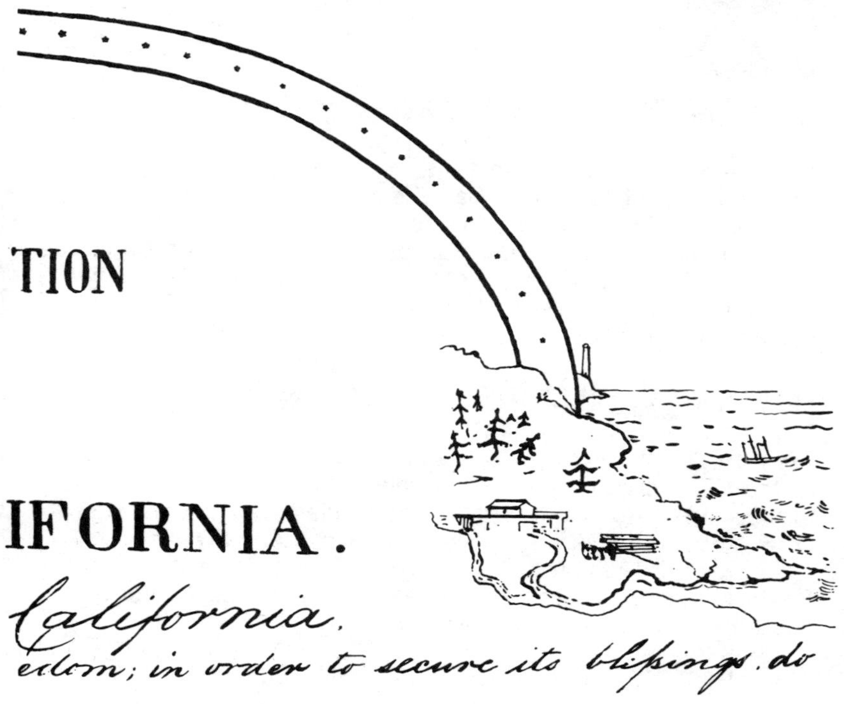

1848 -- Treaty of Guadalupe Hidalgo--Mexico officially ceded California to the United States.

1849 -- California's first constitution.

1850 -- California is admitted to the Union as the 31st state on September 9, 1850.

1869 -- Transcontinental railroad completed--The Southern Pacific Railroad continued its growth and monopolistic practices, later it became known as the "Octopus."

1880 -- California adopts its second constitution--restricting Chinese employment, railroads and corporate officials.

1911 -- An amendment to the State Constitution gives us the tools of direct democracy: recall, referendum and initiative.

1942 -- Beginning of internment, in World II, of Japanese-American citizens.

1978 -- Proposition 13 passed by voters. This property tax limitation initiative helped overtaxed homeowners, but greatly restricted county government.

1990 -- Proposition 140 passed. This term limitation initiative reduced the number of terms that a state legislator could serve and lessened their staffs and pensions.

UNDER THE FLAG OF SPAIN

Juan Rodriguez Cabrillo, in 1542, on a voyage paralleling the California coast, sailed into San Diego Bay and named it "San Miguel." Although the name did not survive, Cabrillo is credited with being the first European to discover California. The Spanish established settlements along the California coastline. These settlements were linked when the mission system was created.

CALIFORNIA MISSIONS

Fray Junipero Serra (known as **Father Serra**) is recognized as the first real colonizer of California. Father Serra, a Catholic Franciscan Priest from Spain, established the first mission (1769) near what is now downtown San Diego. The second mission, near Monterey Bay, is where father Serra is buried. Spain used four types of settlements to colonize California: missions, presidios, pueblos and ranchos.

The ***MISSIONS*** *were Spanish style adobe buildings with high arches, long corridors and red tiled roofs that surrounded a courtyard.* Missions were created for more than religious instruction. They were similar to vocational schools, where the natives could learn a trade and how to care for farms and orchards. Father Serra personally established nine missions, the number later growing to 21.

EL CAMINO REAL *is Spanish for "The King's Highway."* It is the original horseback trail used to travel between missions and from presidio to presidio. The missions were located so that they were only a day's horseback ride from each other. Bells on a staff-shaped post now mark these routes and are often seen on US Route 1 while traveling along the California coast.

PRESIDIOS *were frontier forts.* Most were located at strategic locations, usually at the entrance to a pueblo or port. ***PUEBLOS*** *were clusters of adobe houses, usually including a church, that formed a town or small city.* Among the first settlements were San Jose in 1777 and Los Angeles, "the City of the Angels," in 1781.

MEXICAN RULE 1821 - 1846

Mexico won its independence from Spain in 1821.

Historical note: Mexico repelled a French invasion force on May 5, 1862. ***CINCO de MAYO** (The fifth of May) marks the battle with the French in which Mexico turned back its first foreign invader as an independent country.* Cinco de Mayo is more widely celebrated here than is Mexico's independence from Spain.

In 1833, under the Mexican Secularization Act, Mexico seized the missions and the surrounding lands. They then distributed half the land to the Indians. The missions were stripped of their lands and converted into parish churches.

At the same time, some select, wealthy gentlemen established ranchos. The ***RANCHOS** were large parcels of land given to families of prominence to establish large, un-fenced grazing areas for raising cattle.* Between 1830 and 1845, the number of private ranchos on land grants increased from 50 to 1,045.

CALIFORNIA IS TAKEN FROM MEXICO

The Bear Flag Revolt started in California on June 14, 1846 before anyone realized that the United States had already declared war on Mexico. The ***BEAR FLAG REVOLT** started over the fear that the Mexican government would move against settlers in California.* The revolt began in Sonoma, where General Marino Guadalupe Vallejo was put under house arrest by a band of American settlers who declared an independent "Republic of California." A symbol of this battle was a flag with a bear gazing at a single star. The motto on the flag read:

> **"A bear stands his ground always, and as long as the stars shine we stand for the cause"**

The Bear Flag Revolt was a short-lived event. It ended 22 days later when Mexico surrendered control of Monterey to U.S. forces.

EARLY FLAG

CURRENT FLAG

POPULATION STATISTICS ACCORDING TO U.S. CENSUS

Year	Population	Year	Population
1850 -	92,000	1930 -	5,677,251
1860 -	379,994	1940 -	6,907,387
1870 -	560,247	1950 -	10,586,223
1880 -	864,694	1960 -	15,717,204
1890 -	1,213,398	1970 -	20.1 million
1900 -	1,485,053	1980 -	23.9 million
1910 -	2,377,549	1990 -	30 million
1920 -	3,426,861	2000 -	36 million (estimate)
		2010 -	42 million (projected)

The United States had declared war on Mexico in 1846 over a boundary dispute in Texas. By 1847, U.S. Troops had control of Texas, New Mexico, Arizona and California. The United States and Mexico signed the Treaty of Guadalupe Hidalgo on February 2, 1848. The ***TREATY OF GUADALUPE HIDALGO*** *ended the war with Mexico and allowed the California Republic to become part of the United States.* The treaty honored the earlier Spanish land grants and later Mexican land grants.

GOLD WAS DISCOVERED

On January 24, 1848, gold was discovered by James Wilson Marshall, a carpenter employed by John Sutter to construct a sawmill at Coloma on a branch of the American River. The sound of "Eureka!" was heard around the world. ***EUREKA*** *refers to the gold rush and means "I have found it!"*

The greatest influx of gold hunters was in 1849, hence the new arrivals were given the name "forty-niners." Hysteria about the amount of gold caused California's population to swell, especially around Sacramento, from 15,000 in 1848, to over 92,000 by 1850 and again to 380,000 by 1860. But even after the gold fever broke, people continued to come. The completion of the transcontinental railroad (1869) continued to bring more people to establish or work in merchandising and manufacturing companies.

CALIFORNIA STATEHOOD 1850

In the Fall of 1849, a constitutional convention was held and the new Californians overwhelmingly approved their first California Constitution. It established a state government that is similar to today's state government.

The California constitution included:

Bill of Rights (in the beginning)
Plural executive branch
Legislature (Senate and Assembly)
Elected judicial branch (four levels of courts)
White males 21 years of age could vote
Government documents were printed in
English and Spanish.

The U.S. Congress approved this constitution and California became the 31st state admitted to the Union. *ADMISSION DAY was September 9, 1850, the date California became a state.* There was much concern as to whether California would be admitted as a slave or free state, but the U.S. Congress moved very quickly to make California another non-slave state for the Union.

THE GREAT SEAL OF CALIFORNIA

The constitutional convention of 1849 adopted the "Great Seal of the State of California." Around the top of the ring are 31 stars representing California's position as the 31st state admitted to the Union. The foreground figure represents the Goddess Minerva who, according to Greek mythology, sprang full-grown from the head of Zeus, her father. She symbolizes the political birth of the State of California without having to go through the probation of being a territory.

At her feet is a gold miner and also a grizzly bear feeding on grape vines. The snow-capped peaks of the Sierra Nevada are in the background with the state motto "Eureka," which refers to the gold rush.

The Secretary of State is the keeper of the Great Seal, used to emboss official state documents. A person who misuses or reproduces the Great Seal without permission is guilty of a misdemeanor.

THE RAILROADS (GOOD AND BAD)

The Central Pacific Railroad Company's eventual founders were referred to as the "Big Four." Their last names may still sound familiar today:

Leland Stanford
Collis P. Huntington
Mark Hopkins
Charles Crocker

President Lincoln signed the Pacific Railroad Bill (1862) that called for the simultaneous start of the Central Pacific Railroad in Sacramento and Union Pacific Railroad in Omaha. The bill called for these two railroad lines to receive land and government subsidies based on the miles of rails laid. The extreme wealth and power of the big four railroad barons enabled them to gain a stranglehold on the early economic and political life of California. For 50 years (1860-1910), the railroads were the dominant economic force that shaped California's growth. Thousands of Chinese workers were brought to California to help build the railroads, working under near-slavery conditions. The transcontinental railroad network was completed when the two railroads were joined by the famous "gold spike" at Promontory, Utah in 1869.

But, in the 1890's, things changed for the "octopus," the name given to the railroad companies. William Randolph Hearst, who inherited the San Francisco Examiner newspaper from his father, started an ongoing crusade against the Big Four by publishing critical articles and pointed political cartoons.

CALIFORNIA'S SECOND CONSTITUTION

The ***WORKINGMEN'S PARTY*** *was an anti-railroad group that disapproved of the large number of unemployed Chinese abandoned in the wake of the railroad construction.* Their reform measures,

that were later approved by the state legislature, included: a public school system, an eight-hour work day, land monopoly laws, restrictions on Chinese labor and laws defining the responsibility of corporate directors and officers. The movement was so strong that the *SECOND CALIFORNIA STATE CONSTITUTION (1879) was adopted and later ratified by the voters after a special constitutional convention.*

A CONSTITUTIONAL CONVENTION is an accepted method to alter a state's constitution or to write an entirely new document, which is submitted to the electorate for a ratification vote.

THE CALIFORNIA PROGRESSIVES (REFORMERS)

In the early part of the 20th century, the Southern Pacific Railroad (its new name) was still monopolizing California's politics and manipulating politicians. But the California Progressive party changed this situation. The *PROGRESSIVES were a group of reform-minded Republicans who split from the party to enact permanent changes in the political system that are the basis of the election laws today.*

Hiram Johnson, the new progressive governor, pushed for political reforms. Among the reform measures passed in 1911 were the: initiative, referendum, recall, direct primary, nonpartisan city and county elections and a civil service system. The Progressives introduced direct democracy into the California political system. See Chapter 4 for more details.

The Federal Government: State vs. Federal Powers

In this part of the chapter we look at the two arenas in which California Politics unfolds. The first arena is California's representatives to the federal system: the U.S. Senate and the U.S. House of Representatives. We will also look at the presidency of the United States. The rest of this chapter is devoted to how this federal system is played out on the California political stage and how the state gets money from the federal government.

The second arena is pure Californian: our governor and our state legislature. Every chapter, except this one, will discuss only California political matters.

CERTAIN POWERS ARE FOR THE STATE

The highest power in the United States is the federal government. But certain powers are allowed to be used by the states. The 10th Amendment to the Constitution of the United States reads:

> **"The powers not delegated to the United States by the Constitution, nor prohibited by it to the States, are reserved to the States respectively, or to the people."**

Among other powers reserved solely for the states are the powers to:

1. Establish and control local governments
2. Conduct elections
3. Allow for the formation of business corporations
4. Establish civil and criminal laws
5. Police powers

Of the various powers reserved for the state, police power is probably one of the most important. ***POLICE POWER*** *permits the state to take action to protect the public health, safety, morals and welfare of its citizens.*

Some powers are concurrent. ***CONCURRENT POWERS*** *are powers shared by both the state and the federal government.* Two very important concurrent powers are the ability to tax and to borrow money.

Money from Washington

In the last three decades the federal government has been giving money to the states and local governments to help with certain programs. These financial incentives are the federal government's way of influencing and coaxing each individual

state to do what Washington, D.C. wants it to do. It is a way to redistribute taxes collected by the federal government to the states. The federal government, in the 1960's, began sharing 15% of the nation's budget with the states and local governments and, by 1980, this figure had risen to an all-time high of 23%. The method that the federal government uses to make money available to the states is called grant-in-aid.

GRANT-IN-AID

GRANT-IN-AID is money given from one governmental body to another for a specific purpose. These grants come with strings attached from the U.S. Congress. Most grants require matching funds. *MATCHING FUNDS are federal monies given to the state or local governments that must be matched, dollar for dollar, or they will not be granted.*

Grant-in-aid is disbursed in two different ways: categorical grants and block grants. *CATEGORICAL GRANTS are grants made for a specific purpose or to target a specific program. The restrictions on this type of grant leave the recipient with very little discretion.* Two examples of categorical grants would be programs for AIDS patients and the homeless.

The opposite of a categorical grant is a block grant. A *BLOCK GRANT is the awarding of money for general purposes from one level of government to another.* Of the 400 grants-in-aid available, only 14 are currently block grants. This type of grant allows the recipients the freedom to allocate the money among individual programs. For example, if a block grant is for mass transit, it can be used for buses, trains or construction of stations.

Many of these federal grant-in-aid programs have worked to remove gross inequities among the states. But remember— these programs are highly political. For example, the 1984 Highway Act reduced the amount of money available to states that allowed those under 21 years of age to consume alcoholic beverages.

Within four years, every state in the union had a minimum drinking age of 21.

CALIFORNIA'S PART IN THE U. S. CONGRESS

The ***U.S. CONGRESS*** *is made up of two U.S. Senators from California and 52 California members to the U.S. House of Representatives.* California has the largest contingent to the Congress. California's ability to influence national legislation is high, but their ability to organize as a pro-California coalition is another question. The current number of Democratic and Republican representatives is almost evenly split, making it difficult for them to organize a pro-California coalition.

FEDERAL AND CALIFORNIA LEGISLATURES

Because of the possible confusion between the legislative houses of the United States and California, a U.S. Senator will always have the "U.S." in front of the word "Senator" and a "state senator" will be referred to as such. Similarly, a member of the U.S. House of Representatives must be distinguished from the state assembly to the California legislature in Sacramento. For a complete breakdown of the state legislature, see Chapter 7.

U.S. SENATE (U.S. SENATORS)

A ***U.S. SENATOR*** *is one of two representatives from each state who altogether form the upper chamber of the federal legislature consisting of 100 members.* California can only elect two members to the U.S. Senate. Each U.S. Senator must be at least 30 years of age and have been a U.S. citizen for nine years. A U.S. Senator serves a six-year term. The two U.S. Senators from California may represent the largest concentration of citizens in the U.S., but have only two votes.

U.S. Senators are elected from the entire state. A candidate for the U.S. Senate must spend a large amount of time and money campaigning throughout the state.

An ***INCUMBENT*** *is the person currently occupying a specific elective office.* Our federal system greatly favors the incumbent U.S. Senator and the current U.S. House of Representatives member, because of their name recognition and an already established campaign organization.

Let's Work Together... for California

Can Our Congressional Representatives Work Together?

The ***CALIFORNIA CAUCUS*** *is all the U.S. Representatives from California who form a network to coordinate legislation beneficial to our state.* They are supposed to work together so that legislation beneficial to California is passed. However, they seem to be concentrating their voting power more towards partisan politics rather than our state's interests. What California needs is cooperation. Let's put partisan politics aside and come out with a clear set of objectives that benefit California.

U.S. HOUSE OF REPRESENTATIVES

U.S. CONGRESSIONAL MEMBER *is the term used to address a member of the U.S. House of Representatives.* There are 52 congressional members of the House of Representatives elected from California. Although they receive the same salary as a U.S. Senator ($125,000), they do not enjoy the same recognition due to the fact that there are only two of the latter. In 1992, California added seven congressional members because our population had increased.

California's members to the U.S. House of Representatives (all members serve only a two year term) are generally not known throughout the state because they are elected from districts that are spread throughout the state.

State & Federal Reapportionment

REDISTRICTING MEANS POLITICAL POWER

Redistricting takes place each decade after the U.S. Census is completed. The last census was in 1990 and the next will happen in 2000. ***REDISTRICTING (reapportionment)*** *is the process by which our state legislature redraws the district lines for California's members of the U.S. House of Representatives and at the same time redraws district lines for its own state legislature.*

REDISTRICTING: POWERFUL LEGISLATIVE TOOL

The political party that controls the state legislature has the "assured power" in California to decide how state legislative districts and federal congressional districts are to be drawn. The legislature is obligated to divide these districts in a way that serves the interests of the citizens living there.

Currently the Democratic Party controls the California Senate and the Republican Party the California Assembly. Because the current Republican governor had the power to veto the legislature's plan for redistricting, the legislature could only go so far in fixing the voter pattern within each redrawn district or the governor may reject the plan. This is exactly what happened to the 1990 Census redistricting plan. Since the governor and the legislature could not agree, the California Supreme Court drew the district lines.

The Native Americans, or Indians, were California's first inhabitants. They numbered around 150,000 before the Europeans arrived to "settle" the region. By 1900 there were only around 16,000 Indians left.

The Spanish arrived next. Juan Cabrillo sailed up the west coast and was the first European visitor to California (1542). Fray Junipero Serra established a chain of missions starting in 1769. Each mission was a day's horseback ride from the next. Presidios (frontier forts) were established to protect the missions. Pueblos (small settlements) also sprang up at places like San Jose and Los Angeles.

In 1821, Mexico broke from Spain. Huge land grants in California parceled grazing land into ranchos. California broke from Mexico and became a U.S. possession under the Treaty of Guadalupe Hidalgo in 1847. The next year, gold was discovered at Sutter's Mill in the Sacramento area. Gold fever resulted in a massive population growth that has hardly slowed since the time of the "forty-niners." Statehood followed on September 9, 1850 when the state constitution was approved and California joined the union as the 31st state.

Railroads were the dominant force in the new state's economic growth for fifty years. The "Big Four" of the Central Pacific Railroad (Stanford, Huntington, Hopkins and Crocker) wielded unquestionable political and economic power. The construction of the transcontinental railroad brought thousands of Chinese to California to work under near-slavery conditions. Changes in the California constitution were framed to restrict Chinese labor but they also brought into effect some of the great progressive elements of our state system: free public schools, the eight hour workday, laws governing monopolies and corporations and the tools of direct democracy: recall referendum and initiative. The Progressive Party under Governor Hiram Johnson furthered this progressive movement with more constitutional reforms in 1911.

Police powers, the right to protect the public health, safety, morals and welfare, are held by the state while certain concurrent powers, such as taxing and borrowing money, are shared with the federal government. California has two seats in the United States Senate and 52 congressional seats in the United States House of Representatives. We have more representatives in Congress than any other state.

1. What were the contributing factors that lead to the demise of the California Native Indians?
2. What was the "function" of the mission system in California?
3. What political issues did the second California State Constitution in 1879 change?
4. Explain what powers the 10th Amendment to the Constitution of the United States gives the state of California.
5. What is redistricting and who does it protect?

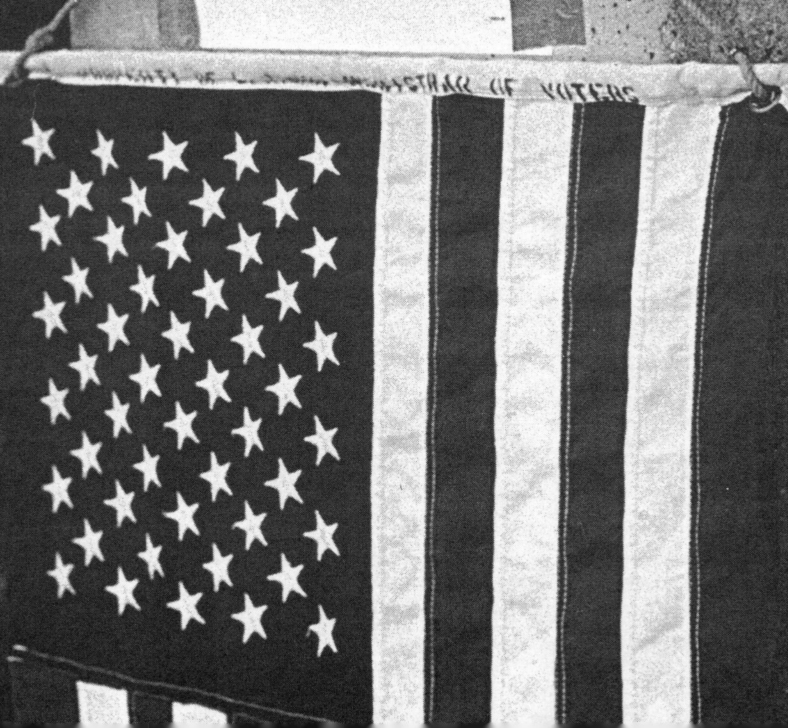
SE
HABLA
ESPAÑOL
POLLING
PLACE

CHAPTER 3 Voters, Primaries & General Elections

WHO MAY VOTE?

You are eligible to register to vote in California if you meet the following criteria:

1. You are 18 years old, or older, by election day.
2. You are a U.S. Citizen.
3. You are a resident of California.
4. You are not in prison or on parole for a felony.
5. You haven't been found incompetent by a judge.

Source: A Guide for Voter Registration in California. Prepared by March Fong Eu, Former Secretary of State. Available from the Sacramento office.

REGISTER TO VOTE (WE ALL ENCOURAGE THIS)

In order to vote you must be a registered voter. A ***REGISTERED VOTER*** *is an eligible voter who has filled out an affidavit of registration and delivered it to the county clerk's office or registrar of voters at least 29 days before an election. A four-day grace period is given for mail-in registration.*

The secretary of state oversees the voting process, but the actual administrating of the voting is a county and city function.

FOR YOUR INFORMATION

The registration of a voter is permanent, unless canceled by the registrar of voters. If you move into a new precinct, change your name or change your political party, you should correct this information with your county registrar of voters as soon as possible. All of the information on your voter registration form is public information that can be obtained by anyone for his or her own personal use.

MUST A PERSON READ ENGLISH TO VOTE?

NO! Prior to 1970, a Californian had to demonstrate that he or she could read the U.S. Constitution in English before being eligible to register. The Federal Voting Rights Act Amendment, as well as certain California Supreme Court decisions, also allows citizens to vote who only speak or write in a language other than English. A person who cannot speak or write may also vote.

Primary Elections

In California the primary election is made up of three different elections, all on the same ballot.

The ***PRIMARY ELECTION*** *includes the following: (1) A direct primary that selects partisan (political party) candidates for statewide offices; (2) A nonpartisan primary that selects county and judicial officials, county party officials and the state superintendent of public instruction; (3) A presidential primary that selects state delegates, from each political party, to their national nominating convention for president and vice president.*

DIRECT PRIMARY

A ***DIRECT PRIMARY*** *is an early election for the purpose of selecting partisan-party candidates from among those nominated. It* *places the final responsibility of candidate selection with the voters, not the political party itself.* A direct primary eliminates the need for a party convention to select the party's candidates for a given office.

CALIFORNIA USES A CLOSED PRIMARY

California has its primary election on the first Tuesday after the first Monday in June of even-numbered years. It is a closed primary. In a *CLOSED PRIMARY, a voter can only receive a ballot for the party in which he or she is registered.* By contrast, some other states have *OPEN PRIMARIES, in which the voters can decide upon arrival at the polls what party ballot they want.*

So if you are a registered Democrat, you receive a Democratic party ballot and can only vote for Democrats in the primary election in June. Registered Republicans only receive a Republican party ballot and, if you "decline to state" your political preference, you can only vote for non-party (nonpartisan) nominees.

CROSS-FILING WAS ABOLISHED

California used to allow cross-filing, but not anymore! *CROSS-FILING allowed a candidate for a partisan public office to run in any political party's primary he or she desired.*

Cross-filing blurred party lines and, over a period of time, weakened the political parties. But now the law has changed and party designation, if any, must appear on the ballot.

NONPARTISAN OFFICES IN THE PRIMARY

A NONPARTISAN PRIMARY is a primary election to nominate a candidate for which no political party may legally nominate a candidate, such as judges, school boards, county and municipal offices and the state superintendent of public instruction. The election of supreme court judges and appellate court judges is handled differently (see Chapter 8 on Courts). A person who wishes to seek the nomination of a nonpartisan office simply declares his or her candidacy and gathers the signatures required to get on the ballot.

A nonpartisan primary election differs greatly from a partisan primary election in one important aspect: A nonpartisan primary candidate who receives a majority vote in a primary election wins the office instantly without the need of going on to a general election. A ***MAJORITY VOTE*** *means that more than fifty percent of the votes cast support one candidate.* If no candidate receives a majority vote in the primary, a run-off between the two individuals with the largest number of votes takes place in the up-coming general election.

THE PRESIDENTIAL PRIMARY

The ***PRESIDENTIAL PRIMARY*** *is the direct election of delegates to the national party conventions that select nominees for the offices of president and vice president of the United States.* The presidential primary is combined with the regular California primary that is held on the first Tuesday after the first Monday in June of each presidential election year (any year evenly divisible by the whole number four). The delegates selected go to the national party convention usually held in July or August.

General Elections

The ***GENERAL ELECTION*** *is the election held throughout the nation on the first Tuesday after the first Monday of November in even-numbered years.* Court decisions and federal laws have made voter qualifications and election days uniform across the country. More people vote in general elections because of the national media visibility of the candidates.

The big distinction is that, in a primary election, the nominee only wins the right to run as the party candidate, whereas in the general election he or she actually wins the office.

WHO VOTES IN CALIFORNIA

Exit polls have shown over and over again that the largest segment of the population that votes has many things in common. Here is what the typical voters in California have in common:

An Earlier California Presidential Primary

California has moved its presidential primary to March 26th, in 1996, instead of the old June date for election years. This will make California a major player in the presidential sweepstakes. Other states have their primary elections in February and March. These states receive a great deal of attention and become the focus of the world's media. Why should the smaller states of Iowa and New Hampshire get most of the recognition?

Since California is the state with the largest population (more than 32 million), it represents 20% of the votes needed to win a party's national primary nomination. California, with a much more culturally diverse population than the rest of the United States, will grab even more world attention. This is a one-time-only experiment, but future legislatures could make the earlier primary permanent.

1. Over 80% are white
2. Most are homeowners, not renters
3. Most voters are older, with no children at home
4. Most have a post-high school education

A high percentage of the younger adults and minorities do not register to vote, or vote, as regularly as the older, white population. But it is only a matter of time until Asians, Hispanics and younger people wake up and join the political process. This group of non-voters can be likened to a sleeping giant just waiting for someone to wake it up and make it aware of its political power.

SPECIAL ELECTIONS

A *SPECIAL ELECTION is usually called by the governor to fill unexpired terms and to decide certain ballot measures.* If there is a vacancy in a U.S. congressional or an open state legislative office, the governor must call for a special election. When a vacancy occurs in a U.S. Senate or U.S. House of Representative's position after the close of the nomination period in the final year of the congressional term, the governor may, at his or her discretion, decline to call a special election and appoint a replacement.

ELECTIONS ARE CONSOLIDATED

CONSOLIDATED ELECTIONS means that the elections for different levels of government are put together on the same ballot on the same election date in order to save money and effort. For example, the presidential primary, on the federal level, is consolidated with the statewide, direct and nonpartisan primary. This only happens once every four years.

The regularly scheduled election dates for each year are:

LOCAL (MUNICIPAL) ELECTION DATES

April (2nd Tuesday of even-numbered years) or **March** (1st Tuesday, after the 1st Monday of odd-numbered years)

STATEWIDE ELECTION DATES

June* (1st Tuesday, after the 1st Monday each year)
November* (1st Tuesday, after the 1st Monday each year)

*** Elections held in June & November of each even-numbered year are considered California's statewide election dates.**

CALIFORNIA VOTERS

TIME SCHEDULE

Registration—ANY TIME (AT LEAST 29 DAYS BEFORE ELECTION)

Primaries—JUNE (FIRST TUESDAY AFTER FIRST MONDAY)

I. Direct Primary (NOMINATING CANDIDATES)

U.S. SENATOR (2), U.S. HOUSE OF REPRESENTATIVES (52), STATE SENATORS (40), STATE ASSEMBLY MEMBERS (80)

II. Nonpartisan Primary (ELECTION AT PRIMARIES)

STATE SUPERINTENDENT OF PUBLIC INSTRUCTION, JUDICIAL AND COUNTY OFFICERS, COUNTY PARTY COMMITTEE MEMBERS

III. Presidential Primary (PRESIDENT)

NATIONAL PARTY CONVENTION DELEGATES

General Elections

NOVEMBER (FIRST TUESDAY AFTER FIRST MONDAY IN EVEN NUMBERED YEARS)

PRESIDENTIAL & GUBERNATORIAL ELECTIONS

MARCH/APRIL (SECOND TUESDAY IN MARCH OR SECOND TUESDAY IN APRIL OR AT THE PRIMARY OR GENERAL ELECTIONS)

COUNTY SUPERVISORS, MAYORS, COUNCIL MEMBERS, TREASURERS, CLERKS, AND OTHERS

Special Elections

ANYTIME (CALLED BY GOVERNOR OR LOCAL GOVERNMENT) UNEXPIRED TERMS :

U.S. SENATORS, U.S. HOUSE OF REPRESENTATIVES, STATE SENATORS, STATE ASSEMBLY MEMBERS

Precincts and Ballots

PRECINCTS AND POLLING PLACES

The county registrar of voters divides the county into voting precincts. A ***PRECINCT*** *is a geographical area made up of a group of voters from a low of 60 to a high of approximately 600, depending on the election and how the registrar groups voters.*

District vs. At-large Elections

A continuing controversy in California involves the at-large versus the district method of electing local government officials. ***AT-LARGE*** *is the process of electing a local government official from a group of candidates whose nominations* ***are not*** *based on where they reside, as is the case with district elections.* Only about 5% of the cities and counties in California use the district method.

With at-large elections, the interests of the whole are put ahead of individual neighborhoods. Being elected at-large does not prohibit the election of qualified candidates from the same residential area; the best qualified should be allowed to serve.

District election supporters claim that allowing more than one officeholder per neighborhood is unfair, mainly because the officeholders generally reside in the most affluent areas.

Each precinct has a precinct board. The board is made up of one inspector, two judges and three clerks. Each board member must be a voter from that precinct or a precinct in that area. Any voter may apply to be one of these precinct workers, who usually <u>volunteer</u> for the position. You, as students, can gain important political insight from being a precinct volunteer during a long election day. The ***POLLING PLACE (POLLS)*** *is the location within a precinct where the voting takes place.* Schools and public buildings are popular polling places because these types of structures are available free of charge. A polling place can be just about anywhere, but not in a bar or liquor store.

ELECTION DAY

On election day, the polls open at 7am and close at 8pm. This makes for a 13-hour voting period.

ABSENTEE BALLOT

An *ABSENTEE BALLOT is a ballot that is sent to you, before the election, if you cannot vote in person at the polling place on election day. It must be received back before the close of the polls.* You must apply, in writing, in order to receive an absentee ballot.

The absentee ballot has become very popular in recent years. In many campaigns part of the campaign strategy is to send absentee ballot request forms to anyone who supports a particular candidate whether it is requested or not.

CALIFORNIA DOES NOT PURGE

A *VOTER PURGE is when the registrar of voters goes through the list of registered voters on a systematic basis and eliminates certain voters from the list.* The usual reason is that the voter has not voted in the last general election. In California there is no annual purge of the voter registration roster.

CALIFORNIA'S BALLOT FORMS

California uses a long ballot form. A *LONG BALLOT is a complete list of the offices, items and propositions to be decided upon by the voters.* We have eleven state executives to elect, other than the governor, as well as judges, county officials, city officials plus ballot propositions, bond issues and maybe a charter amendment or two. We may complain about the length of the ballot, but we are reluctant to give up on the privilege of deciding many issues ourselves.

California uses the office-block type of ballot. An *OFFICE-BLOCK BALLOT presents all the competing candidates, by office, throughout the ballot.* The voter makes his or her choice in an office-by-office manner. In contrast, some other states use a *PARTY-COLUMN BALLOT, which lists the candidates party-by-party.* At the top of a party column ballot is a box

where a single mark will cast a vote for all of the party candidates. In California, however, it is difficult to vote a party ticket. The office-block ballot forces voters to think of candidates as individuals rather than as part of a partisan ballot ticket.

Chapter Summary

Everything in California politics is structured around our two major political parties, the democrats and republicans, although minor political parties play an important role, often bringing new issues and ideas into the mainstream. When you register to vote, you are asked to choose a party which is a factor in every step of the election process.

In California we use a “direct primary” to select our ballot candidates for major state offices. A direct primary allows the voters to pick their party's candidate from a slate of those nominated by the party. The candidates from each party who win the primary election then go up against each other in the general election. California holds a “closed” primary, where each voter receives only the ballot of the party in which they are already registered. In some states with an “open” primary, voters can decide at the polls which party ballot they want.

In a presidential primary, the voters do not directly choose their party candidate. Instead, voters elect the delegates to the party convention, and these delegates choose the party candidate. If you want to see a certain candidate represent your party on the presidential ballot, you must vote for a delegate pledged to that candidate in the primary.

A non-partisan primary is held to select candidates for offices that are supposed to be non-party oriented, such as judges, school boards and the state superintendent of instruction. In such an election, if one of the candidates receives more than half the votes, he or she wins the office immediately. If not, the two leading candidates face a run-off. In the run-off election the person with the most votes wins.

A general election is held every other year in California (on the first Tuesday after the first Monday in November in even-numbered years). In presidential election years, voters select from the party candidates nominated by delegates at the party convention the previous summer. In gubernatorial election years, voters choose from party candidates elected directly in the primary election. Congressional candidates, senators, state representatives, judges, school boards, city councils—all types of elected positions that are available— as well as ballot initiatives, will be included in a consolidated election every two years.

A special election is an election, other than the scheduled primary or general elections, called at any time, by the governor. These are generally called to fill an office vacancy or to decide an important ballot measure.

The county registrar of voters divides the county into voting precincts. Each precinct has its precinct board (one inspector, two judges, three clerks) and a polling place where the voting takes place. Voters may vote by mail with an absentee ballot, which must be sent in before the polls close. On election day in California the polls open at 7am and close at 8pm.

1. How is a closed primary different from an open primary?

2. What is the presidential primary?

3. California has more registered Democrats or Republicans?

4. What are the main reasons for voter apathy in California?

5. Discuss the three main types of ballots.

CALIFORNIA

CHAPTER 4

Direct Democracy

In 1911, amendments to the state constitution gave us the three basic tools of direct democracy:

THE RECALL,
THE INITIATIVE AND
THE REFERENDUM.

These three tools removed much of the partisan politics from government and gave California voters the right to help set public policy. Hiram Johnson was the father of California's direct democracy.

The Father of California Democracy

Governor Hiram Johnson "The Progressive Reformer"
1911-1917 (two terms) Republican

Chapter 4

Hiram Johnson, the "Progressive" Republican, was overwhelmingly voted into the governor's office because he, as did a majority of voters, disliked the political power of the railroad monopoly that had been building for decades. His goal was to "get the Southern Pacific Railroad out of politics."

A large number of Progressive Republicans and Democrats joined together to support the progressive idea and cause. *A **PROGRESSIVE** is usually thought of as favoring the restriction of corporate influence in politics and expanding the citizens' participation in politics, while protecting the environment and improving working and living conditions.*

The Progressive Reformers saw political parties as the instrument that the Southern Pacific Railroad monopoly had used to dominate the state government for over four decades.

The Progressive Reforms That Changed California ... Hiram Johnson

1909 REFORMS

The direct primary law was enacted. This meant that candidates for public office must be nominated at a special election called a direct primary, not at a party convention, which had been the practice. This eliminated the "behind closed door" selection of party candidates.

1911 REFORMS

The Railroad Commission, which regulated the railroads and all the utilities, was increased from three to five members who were **now appointed by the governor** instead of being elected.

The direct democracy initiative, referendum and recall became part of the state constitution. Now the voters could actually reverse laws and even make laws themselves or vote an official out of office.

Judicial and school board elections became nonpartisan.

Women obtained the right to vote. The U.S. Constitution was not amended to include women's suffrage until 1920.

Office-Block Ballot was introduced. This requires the voters to vote for each office separately.

1913 REFORMS

City, County, and local special district elections became nonpartisan.

The leadership and operations of political parties was defined in detail by law.

Cross-filing was permitted by candidates, thus allowing them to run for the same office of each party in the primary election. Cross-filing was abolished by governor Earl Warren.

Hiram Johnson is called the father of California Democracy.

The progressives' main objective was to weaken the political party system in California. The mostly positive effects of these reforms are still with us today.

3 Tools of Direct Democracy

(Recall, Referendum and Initiative)

THE RECALL

The *RECALL is a procedure whereby any California state elected official can be removed from public office, before the completion of his or her term, by a majority vote.* Any elected official may be recalled for any reason, but the procedure does take time and effort.

California's two U.S. Senators and fifty-two members of the U.S. House of Representatives are exempt from recall because they hold federal offices, which have different removal procedures.

THE RECALL PETITION

If you do not like the kind of job a public official is doing, you must circulate a petition and get the required number of voter signatures for a recall vote. The exact number of signatures varies with the type of position the official holds.

STATEWIDE OFFICE: To recall an official who holds a statewide office, the recall petition must contain signatures equal to 12% of the votes cast for that position in the last election. In addition, the voter signatures must come from at least five counties, and number no less than one percent of the votes cast for the office in that county.

NON-STATEWIDE OFFICE: The recall petition must contain signatures equal to at least 20 percent of the number of votes cast for that position in the last election.

LOCAL LEVEL: On the local level, many recall petitions have obtained the required number of signatures and forced a recall vote. It is difficult, however, to initiate a recall for statewide offices and large districts because of the large number of signatures required. A recall petition does, however, get the public's attention. In the past, there have been unsuccessful statewide recall petition drives against Governor Ronald Reagan, Governor Jerry Brown and Chief Justice Rose Bird.

HOW DOES A RECALL WORK?

The recall petition must state the grounds for removal. It can be as simple as a statement that the individual is not doing his or her job. Public officials need not do anything illegal to be recalled.

The recall petition must be filed with the California secretary of state within a given time period, the maximum being 160 days, of being circulated. If the required number of valid signatures has been obtained, the governor must call for a recall election within 180 days after the secretary of state has certified the accuracy of the petition. The recall ballot is divided into two distinct parts: First, the voters must decide the simple question:

"Shall ____________ be removed from the office of _________________by recall? Vote YES or NO."

Also included are the charges against the public official and the incumbent's own statement in defense of these charges.

A majority "yes" vote will remove the public official from office. Second on the recall ballot is a list of candidates from which the voters will choose a replacement. All that is needed by a new candidate is a plurality (the most votes) of the votes cast.

If the vote is "no" in the recall election, the incumbent remains in office and the recall effort has failed.

The incumbent is now protected for at least six months because no new recall petition can be initiated until six months after the last recall election.

In addition, the state reimburses the incumbent for all election expenses if the recall election fails.

Do not confuse recall with impeachment. Recall is initiated by the voters for any reason. ***IMPEACHMENT*** *is conducted by the state legislature to remove an official from office for a serious violation of the law.*

LOCAL OFFICIAL RECALLS

Local governments set their own requirements for recall elections under the guidelines handed down by our state legislature. For example, no local government recall may require more petition signatures than an amount equal to 25 percent of the votes cast at the last election for that office. The legislature further requires that city recall elections not have a successor section on a recall ballot. The city council either appoints a new official or the voters will choose the new official at the next election.

REFERENDUM (BY PETITION)

A ***REFERENDUM (BY PETITION)*** *is the process of suspending the implementation of a law passed by the legislature (with the approval of the governor or over his or her veto) until it can be voted on by the electorate.* Do not confuse this with the compulsory referendum.The ***COMPULSORY REFERENDUM*** *automatically requires voters at an election to approve a constitutional amendment, charter or bond issue before it can become law.*

The referendum by petition, which prevents a statute from becoming law, requires the signatures of at least 5 percent of registered voters who cast votes for governor in the last election. The secretary of state certifies that the petition has the required number of signatures and is submitted on time (within 90 days after enactment of the bill at a regular session and 91 days after a special session). If the referendum petition qualifies, the law is not enforceable until after the next election, where the voters have a chance to formally accept or reject the new law.

Since the enactment of referendum by petition in California, a vote has only been called thirty-nine times and, of those, only twenty-five laws have been repealed. On the other hand, over 180 initiatives have been placed before the voters for their acceptance. The last referendum to be placed on the ballot was in June, 1982, when the Republican minority disagreed with the Democratic-controlled legislature over the Reapportionment Act of 1980. So, by the 1982 elections, voters had placed three related referendum measures on the June ballot. When all three were approved by the voters, the plan for redistricting (U.S. House Representatives, congressional and state legislative districts) was rejected.

DIRECT INITIATIVE

The people of California have another wonderful power; they can make laws without the help of the legislature or the governor through a process known as the direct initiative. *A DIRECT INITIATIVE is a process by which the people draft a proposal or constitutional amendment and acquire enough voter signatures to place the issue on the ballot, where it can be decided by all California voters.* The direct initiative can be on any topic, but must be limited to a "single subject." The governor has no veto power over a direct initiative.

INITIATIVES ARE POPULAR

The longer 150 day qualification period is the key to why so many initiatives are put before the voters. If a trade group, association or some other type of interest group has the desire, it can usually put an initiative before the people by hiring professionals to circulate the initiative petitions. Today one can hire a company just to gather initiative signatures. They usually charge the initiative sponsors from 80 cents to $1.25 for each signature.

PROPOSITIONS ARE GIVEN NUMBERS

The secretary of state gives an initiative or a referendum a proposition number as it meets the necessary qualification requirements for the ballot. A *PROPOSITION is a qualified ballot measure that is given a number from one of these three sources: (1)* ***referendum petition*** *- prevents laws from going into effect (2)* ***compulsory referendums*** *- legislatively approved constitutional amendments and bond issues must always be approved by the voters and (3)* ***direct initiatives*** *- people-approved petitions that can put any issue on the ballot for voter approval.* To avoid confusion with past and current ballot measures, a law was passed to consecutively number propositions starting with the 1982 general election and running in twenty-year cycles. The next cycle will start in 2002.

VOTER BALLOT PAMPHLETS

A *VOTER BALLOT PAMPHLET is a booklet sent before the election to each voter explaining propositions and ballot measures.* Different positions and issues on the statewide ballot are presented by the secretary of state while the city and county clerks help clarify local ballot measures. The secretary of state states:

> "Many rights and responsibilities go along with citizenship. Voting is one of the most important, as it is the foundation on which our democratic system is built. Read carefully all of the measures and all related information contained in this pamphlet. Referendums, legislative propositions and citizen-sponsored initiatives are designed specifically to give us, the electorate, the opportunity to influence the laws which regulate us all."

INITIATIVE REFORM

The rejection by voters of so many ballot initiatives in the general election of November, 1990, may have opened the door to possible changes in California's initiative process. The question is: are we really ready to change our initiative system?

California voters may not be as dumb as some professional signature-gathering firms think. Have some self-generating initiative organizations gone too far by cranking out too many new initiative campaigns? Interest groups that saw the initiative process fail to get their legislation passed by the voters are instead looking to lobbying the legislature as an answer.

The biggest complaints refer to the initiative qualification requirements. Grassroots groups with little money to spend can't get their propositions to the voter.

Other critics want more disclosure of the interests and political forces supporting or opposing initiatives. Some want to simplify the ballot so that the average voter can read the initiative once and understand it. Good Luck!

During the "progressive" period when Hiram Johnson was governor of California (1911-1917), sweeping reforms were made in the state election laws, empowering voters with a more direct form of democracy than was previously enjoyed. The direct primary was created, allowing voters from each party to choose their party candidates for major state offices rather than relying on the traditional party convention. Certain local, judicial and school board seats became nonpartisan. Women received the right to vote in California (although the federal government didn't catch up until 1920). The office-block ballot was introduced, requiring voters to vote for each office separately, rather than voting for an entire party slate with a single stroke. But the most important progressive reform of this period was the creation of the recall, referendum and initiative.

The recall is a procedure by which a state official may be removed from office by a vote of the people. This is not impeachment, where an officeholder is removed for a violation of the law. A recall may be based only on public dissatisfaction. A recall petition is circulated and must be signed by a percentage of the voters (this number varies depending on the office). After a maximum period of 160 days of circulation, if the petition has the proper number of signatures, the governor must call for a recall election. The public is asked to vote "yes" or "no" to the recall and to choose a replacement from a list of candidates. The replacement with the most votes will finish out the term. If the public votes "no" to the recall, the officeholder is safe for at least six months, then a new recall can be initiated. In local elections there is no successor section on the recall ballot. The successor is either appointed by the city council or the office remains vacant until the next election.

A referendum allows the public to block an unwanted law from taking effect. A petition (signed by at least five percent of the registered voters who cast votes for governor in the previous election) must be presented to the secretary of state within 90 days of the enactment of the bill making it unenforceable until after the next election, where the voters may formally reject or accept it.

The direct initiative process allows voters to enact laws for themselves. An initiative is a proposed law or state constitutional amendment initiated by the people. A petition with the proper number of signatures will place an initiative on the ballot for the people to decide in the next election. Initiatives and referendums appear on the ballot as propositions with a number assigned to each by the secretary of state.

1. Why is Hiram Johnson referred to as the father of democracy in California?
2. What group benefits the most from the recall, the initiative and the referendum?
3. Can you think of an instance when the recall may be a bad idea and not in the best interest of democracy?
4. Have the people in California come to rely too heavily on the initiative process?
5. Why do you think there is a 150-day limit to gather signatures for an initiative or referendum?

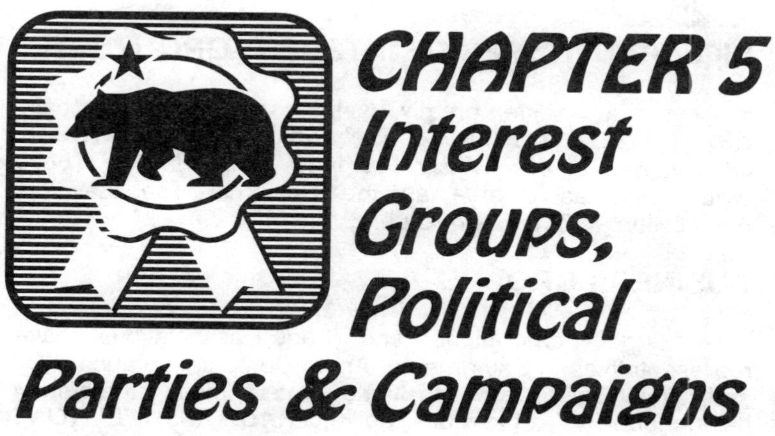

CHAPTER 5 Interest Groups, Political Parties & Campaigns

Interest Groups

We have a large state that is very diverse. It is an amazing society of varying interests and ideas. But all interest groups have one thing in common: they want California's elected officials to know how they feel about their pet issues. It is the stated purpose of interest groups to influence people in such a way that the interest groups point of view will be accepted.

An ***INTEREST GROUP*** *is an organized group having a common interest that attempts to persuade others to see its point of view.* Its objective is to have public policy makers embrace its goals and ideas. For example, the California Association of Realtors is made up of over 125,000 real estate brokers and salespeople who foster the concept of home ownership, and work to protect their sales commissions.

Small groups can have much more of a political impact on legislation if they join forces. The League of California Cities, for example, maintains offices, libraries, researchers and several lobbyists at a fraction of what the cost would be if each city tried to represent its own interest. Almost every city in the state is a member.

DIFFERENT TYPES OF INTEREST GROUPS

Interest groups differ greatly as to money, size and goals. ***PRIVATE AGENDAS*** *are specific objectives set by, in this case, an interest group in order to help it accomplish a specific goal.* These groups are as diverse as the California Trial Lawyers Association and the Sierra Club.

BUSINESS GROUPS

Most large corporations and trade associations have representatives in Sacramento. Apple Computer, Standard Oil and other California-based firms protect their interests by having lobbyists in the state capitol. ***TRADE ASSOCIATIONS*** *are organizations made up of similar businesses whose goal is the promotion of their common interests.* Their goal is straightforward; they want to stay in business by continuing to provide goods or services to the consumer and, at the same time, make a profit. The California Chamber of Commerce represents many different types of firms, but other trade associations represent specific types of businesses, like the California Manufactures Association or the California Retailers Association.

DEMOGRAPHIC INTEREST GROUPS

Gays and Lesbians are good examples of demographic interest groups, although many of their members may not think of themselves as such. ***DEMOGRAPHIC INTEREST GROUPS*** *are groups of people who share characteristics such as income, age and education.* Although they have made great strides for equality in recent years, as a group they have not fully attained their desired objectives. In the area of AIDS treatment and research, they have done a fine job of educating the general public to the fact that it is a disease of the general population, not just the homosexual population.

SINGLE ISSUE GROUPS

Some groups are formed to publicize only one particular issue, and will eventually disappear after that issue has been settled. ***SINGLE ISSUE INTEREST GROUPS*** *consist of people who have a particular interest in one subject and will fight for their cause until*

UNIONS, CORPORATIONS & PROFESSIONAL ASSOCIATIONS

1. **BUSINESS**
   California Chamber of Commerce, California Manufacturers Association, California Bankers Association, California Retailers Association, California Association of Realtors

2. **AGRICULTURE**
   California Farm Bureau Federation, Agricultural Council of California, United Farm Workers

3. **LABOR (UNIONS)**
   California State Employees Association, California Teamsters, Public Affairs Council, California Labor Federation

4. **PROFESSIONAL ASSOCIATIONS**
   California Medical Association, State Bar of California

5. **EDUCATION**
   Association of California School Administrators, California School Boards Association, California Teachers Association, California Federation of Teachers

6. **GOVERNMENT**
   County Supervisors Association, League of California Cities

7. **IDEOLOGICAL ORGANIZATIONS**
   American Civil Liberties Union (ACLU), Common Cause, John Birch Society

8. **RACIAL, ETHNIC OR RELIGIOUS ORGANIZATIONS**
   National Association for the Advancement of Colored People (NAACP), Mexican-American Political Association (MAPA), California Catholic Conference

9. **PUBLIC UTILITIES**
   Pacific Gas & Electric Company, General Telephone

10. **MISCELLANEOUS**
    League of Women Voters, California Tax Payers Association, Sierra Club, Girl Scouts, Boy Scouts

it is settled. Pro-Choice and Pro-Life protesters are just two examples of this category of groups.

LOBBYISTS

Interest groups hire men and women to represent them in our state capital, Sacramento. These people are referred to as lobbyists.

A ***LOBBYIST*** *is a person, acting for specific interest groups, who tries to influence the introduction of legislation and the votes taken on bills in the legislature.* Sometimes lobbyists are referred to as the "third house of the legislature," because they have as much influence over legislation as the assembly and the senate.

WHAT MAKES A SUCCESSFUL LOBBYIST?

Some people may be surprised to find that money, gifts and expensive meals are not the tools used by a successful lobbyist. Lobbyists are not usually loud, but are pleasant and non-offensive. A good lobbyist uses "the soft sell approach" by convincing the official that it is important for him or her to listen. A smart lobbyist is well organized, direct and succinct in his or her presentation. The golden rule is never make a legislator look bad or uninformed.

In Sacramento, where most law-making is done by committee, it is best for the lobbyist to schedule, with the legislator's office, a one or two minute walking meeting between committee meetings.

This lobbying technique is best described by the term "shmooze." ***SHMOOZE*** *is the term used by lobbyists to describe the art of discussing business in a casual, social manner.*

CROWD LOBBYING

CROWD LOBBYING *is the practice of mobilizing large numbers of people to attend organized rallies timed to influence a decision or specific legislation.* The group, if successful, will draw news media attention and attain free publicity for its cause.

Political Parties

CALIFORNIA'S POLITICAL PARTIES

A ***POLITICAL PARTY*** *is a large organization of voters who have similar views and band together to gain more power.* Because of our primary elections and the large number of nonpartisan local government positions, the California political party machinery is not as strong as it is in other states.

A recognized political party is entitled to place its candidates' names on the primary ballot. If a political party registers a number equal to at least one percent of the total votes cast in the last gubernatorial election (approximately 80,000) that party will be recognized by the secretary of state.

League of Women Voters

The ***LEAGUE OF WOMEN VOTERS*** *is a nonprofit, nonpartisan volunteer group that educates voters in the areas of issues and public problems.* The League is especially helpful in analyzing complicated ballot measures so that the public can understand the real issues behind a proposition. It is one of the few interest groups that presents its analysis to the general public in a straightforward, impartial manner. This group is also to be applauded for sponsoring debates between candidates in the interest of voter education. Its main goal is to inform the voter. The state organization is listed below, but there are local chapters throughout California.

League of Women Voters of California
926 J Street, #1000
Sacramento, CA 95814

Our hats are off to the League of Women Voters for their dedication and integrity.

The political parties recognized in California are:

American Independent
Democratic
Green*
Peace and Freedom
Republican
Libertarian

*** party that stresses environmental issues.**

After initial recognition by the secretary of state, an organization must maintain a membership equal to at least 2 percent of the total votes cast in the last gubernatorial election or lose its legal existence.

DEMOCRATS AND REPUBLICANS

Of course, the two major political parties are the Republicans (GOP) and the Democrats (Demos). Most voters in California are either Democrats or Republicans, but it is very common to cross party lines in the privacy of the voting booth. *TICKET-SPLITTING is when a person votes for different political parties, depending on the office.* For example, people may vote for a Republican governor and a Democratic lieutenant governor, a Republican attorney general , just as voters did in the 1994 general election.

POLITICAL LABELS

A *CONSERVATIVE is a person, or philosophy, that tends to favor established traditions and resist change.* We often speak of conservatives as being to the "right" and liberals to the "left." In American politics, conservatives tend to identify with the Republican Party but a person may also be thought of as a conservative Democrat if he or she identifies with the "right" on certain issues.

A *LIBERAL is a person, or philosophy, that tends to favor political reform or progress and is open to ideas which challenge established traditions.* In American politics, liberals tend to identify with the Democratic Party, however, a person could see himself as a liberal or "moderate" Republican.

Labels such as "conservative" and "liberal" are useful in providing a general idea of where a person stands on certain issues. In reality, however, many or most individuals will fluctuate greatly between these positions, depending on the issue.

STATE CENTRAL COMMITTEE

Each recognized political party has a State Central Committee and a County Central Committee. The *STATE CENTRAL COMMITTEE is made up of partisan office holders, nominees, appointees and other minor party officials.* It does not represent the rank-and-file party member.

Each party has large state central committees that are broken down into several parts. The *EXECUTIVE COMMITTEE of each party is a small group of high party officials who meet often to conduct party business in the party name.*

The state central committees adopt resolutions, coordinate fund raising and encourage party enthusiasm. Actual campaigning is done by each individual candidate's organization and any helpful interest groups. The state central committee's effectiveness is minimal because of California's political traditions and our state's large size.

COUNTY CENTRAL COMMITTEE

A *COUNTY CENTRAL COMMITTEE is the county political party group elected by popular vote from assembly districts.* Additional members are party nominees from within the district. The Los Angeles area, which forms one of the largest groups, has over three hundred members on the county committee. County party committees have the job of helping candidates with their campaigns, but like the state committees, they have little effect. Besides, a recent statute has prohibited California political parties from endorsing a candidate before the primary election. Our state laws discourage political parties from having a strong and effective state and county representation.

POLITICAL REFORM ACT (PROPOSITION 9)

The ***POLITICAL REFORM ACT*** *was instituted to oversee more than 100,000 candidates for state and local government, their campaign funds and the activities of lobbyists.* This proposition ensures that state ballot pamphlets will be an independent, useful document sent to each voter, and that laws or practices unfairly favoring incumbents will be abolished. To achieve these goals, the political reform act provides the following:

1. Conflict of interest rules for government officials.
2. Disclosure requirements for candidates, committees, lobbyists and public officials.
3. Nonpartisan ballot pamphlets that analyze and present the actual text of existing laws and proposed changes.

THE FAIR POLITICAL PRACTICES COMMISSION *is a five-member, bipartisan state panel responsible for the administration and enforcement of the Political Reform Act.* The commission may impose direct fines of $2,000 and higher fines through civil suits. All fines are paid into the state treasury, not the agency itself.

No Workplace Smoking

The 1995 smoking ban prohibits any smoking in the workplace, from restaurants and offices to factories and warehouses. Bars may permit smoking. State health experts must draft health standards by 1997 or smoking in bars will be phased out by the turn of the century.

Meanwhile, smoke-related diseases go on killing up 500,000 people each year. Proposition 188, sponsored by Philip Morris (nation's largest tobacco company), would have limited the workplace ban—But it was voted down. This was a good example of how a corporation or industry with unlimited funds can have self-serving propositions placed on the ballot.

Endorsements & PAC's (Political Action Committees)

An *ENDORSEMENT is an official show of support to a candidate from an important source.* Endorsements come from interest groups, celebrities, newspapers, other political leaders and state or county political committees. Endorsements for nonpartisan races were prohibited in 1986 by a constitutional amendment.

In a campaign, real political muscle comes from the ability of a candidate to obtain crucial endorsements and generate campaign contributions especially from PAC's. ***PAC's (Political Action Committees)** are subgroups within large organizations, such as corporations, trade groups, unions and grass roots groups that contribute campaign funds to candidates who support their political view.* It is much easier for a candidate to build a campaign "war chest" from PAC's because large contributions are granted with little effort and they may often include a powerful endorsement.

ELECTION LAWS

In 1991 several new election laws went into effect. They are:

Legislators cannot receive any gift over $250.

Members of state boards and commissions are now subject to the maximum $250 honorarium and limit on gifts.

Legislators are now, for the first time, prohibited from voting on legislation that would be a conflict of interest.

Legislators and members of state boards and commissions are prohibited from lobbying the legislature for at least one year after leaving office.

Campaigns

POLITICAL CAMPAIGNS

Strategy is the key to every well run political campaign. A *CAMPAIGN STRATEGY is a well thought-out tactical plan with winning an election as its goal. This is accomplished by identifying the audience, the message, the delivery and timing while considering the campaign resources.*

The most important element of a good campaign strategy is to develop a good campaign message. The *CAMPAIGN MESSAGE is the theme of the person or the issue that the campaign will attempt to communicate to voters.* The complex issues of a campaign must be reduced down to a simple message that sets the candidate apart from all others.

PAST ELECTIONS OFFER VOTER PATTERNS

VOTER TARGETING is the deliberate attempt on the part of a campaign to identify the precincts or election districts in which to consolidate its effort in order to win. Voter targeting uses past voter patterns and turnouts as the best indicator of future voting patterns for the same precinct. Precincts that have not been committed to a particular political party are called swing voters.

The *SWING VOTERS are the individual voters who have not committed themselves to a particular political party, issue or candidate but, if presented with an appealing campaign message, may vote for that issue or candidate.* These voters should be targeted the most because they may produce the biggest voter switch with the least campaign cost and effort.

A VOTER LIST is the list of registered voters by name, address, party affiliation and, in California, phone numbers that is supplied for a small charge, precinct by precinct, to the purchaser from the county registrar of voters. Not only can individuals or campaigns buy voter lists, but they can also buy precinct results of past elections with a list that identifies who voted in that particular election. But relax, they can not tell anyone how a person actually voted!

Campaign Laws in California

LIMITATIONS ON CONTRIBUTIONS

California campaign laws impose the following contribution limitations for all California election candidates:

$1,000 for individuals;
$2,500 for political committees; and
$5,000 for broad-based political committees and political parties.

Note: Court cases have invalidated the limitations on contributions to candidates in all but "special elections." All or part of these limitations may be reinstated at any time.

CALIFORNIA POLITICAL REFORM ACT

All California candidates and political committees must file a periodic campaign statement listing information regarding financial contributions and expenditures. It is filed with the Fair Political Practices Commission in Sacramento. The report must be signed by the filer, under penalty of perjury, confirming that it is true and correct. In addition, all advertising must identify the sponsor and no contributions over $100 can be anonymous.

LOCAL CAMPAIGN ORDINANCES (LAWS)

Local government can adopt its own campaign laws in addition to the state laws. Some cities and counties have: prohibited corporations from contributing limited contribution, amounts and required additional campaign statements.

FEDERAL ELECTION CAMPAIGN ACT

The Federal Election Campaign Act only applies to people running for a federal office. This law requires these candidates to file periodic public reports disclosing financial facts about campaign contributions and expenditures. The law also sets limits on the amount of money that can be contributed by individuals at $1,000 and may go as high as $5,000 for groups. Copies of these reports can be examined at the office of the Federal Election Commission in Washington, D.C..

Interest groups consist of people with common goals who organize together in an effort to influence public policy making. These groups come in all sizes and types, organized around many different issues: political, economic, cultural and social. Small, local groups will often band together on a statewide basis to wield more clout.

Interest groups often engage professional lobbyists to represent them. Lobbyists are a big part of the political process in Sacramento, building relationships with lawmakers and persuading lawmakers to support legislation favorable to the groups they represent.

Most politicians align themselves with either of the two major political parties, Democrats or Republicans. Along with the American Independent, Green, Peace and Freedom, and Libertarian Parties, these are the six official parties currently on the state ballot. The Republican party is generally viewed as more conservative than the Democrats, tending to resist radical change in favor of more established traditions and values. The Democratic party is perceived as being more liberal, favoring reform and being more open to new ideas. Each party has its own internal structure including a central committee, made up of officeholders and party officials throughout the state, and an executive committee of highly placed party officials that decides policy. Political parties in California don't actually run a candidate's campaign but they do play a major advisory and organizational role.

A great effort is made to keep elections fair. The Political Reform Act (Proposition 9) places controls on candidates, lobbyists and campaign funds. This law is enforced by the bipartisan Fair Political Practices Commission.

Successful political campaigns are based on careful planning and a sound campaign strategy. The campaign message often must be very simple and straight-forward in order to capture the imagination of the voting public. Voter targeting involves identifying key election districts that should be emphasized in campaigning. Swing voters are those who might be persuaded either way on an issue, depending on the appeal of the campaign message.

Class Discussion

1. Is it true that only large business corporations form interest groups?
2. Is it true that interest groups only pull America apart and offer the citizens nothing?
3. Do trade associations only protect the weak?
4. Is it true that the third parties will take on the Democrats and the Republicans soon?
5. Is it true that California has no campaign laws?

CHAPTER 6 The Executive Branch

Executive Branch

The *GOVERNOR OF CALIFORNIA is the chief executive officer of the state government, and because of California's prominence, he or she is also an influential figure in national politics.* The governor, however, does not act alone. California uses a plural executive system. The California *PLURAL EXECUTIVE system is one that consists of the governor and eleven other elected officials* (See next page). Each of the other eleven members of the plural executive runs a separate part of the state government. This is different from the federal government, where more power is concentrated in the hands of a single chief executive. The voters decide who holds these positions, and quite often they are from a different political party than the governor's. All California plural executives:

1) serve four-year terms;
2) term starts 1st Monday after January 1st;
3) have a two-term limit;
4) are subject to recall and impeachment;
5) vacancies filled by the governor.

The balance of the governor's administration is made up mostly of political appointees. These appointees include the governor's cabinet, staff, a large diverse number of agencies, departments and various boards and commissions. The governor is responsible and accountable to the people for the performance of every member of the administration.

Executive Branch Officials

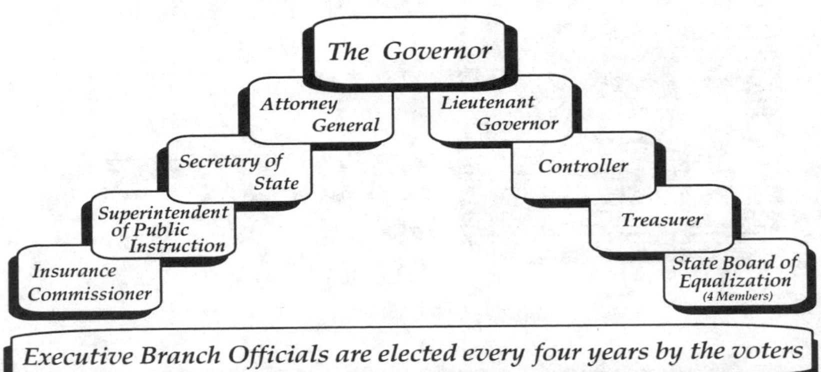

The ***ORDER OF SUCCESSION*** *is the descending order of who assumes the governor's office in the event of death, resignation, removal or disability.* The order of succession for the governor of California is:

1) Lieutenant Governor
2) President Pro Tempore of the Senate
3) Speaker of the Assembly
4) Secretary of State
5) Attorney General
6) Treasurer
7) Controller

If there is a question as to the governor's competence, an appointed commission petitions the State Supreme Court for its determination.

The Office of Governor

Candidates for governor must meet these state requirements:

1. Citizen of the United States
2. Qualified to vote
3. California resident for at least 5 years immediately preceding the election.

GUBERNATORIAL POWERS

GUBERNATORIAL refers to anything having to do with the governor. The gubernatorial powers are those held by the chief executive of the state. They include the following:

1. Ceremonial and Political Leader
2. Appointment Power
3. Judicial Influence
4. Commander-In-Chief of the State Militia
5. Legislative Leader

CEREMONIAL AND POLITICAL PARTY LEADER

The governor is the world representative of California and its citizens. Ceremonial duties include ribbon-cutting, greeting world leaders and other celebrations. In addition to running the executive branch, the governor is also the leader of his or her political party, lending strength and prestige to that party. Also, the governor can exercise influence by making appointments, nominations and shaping the direction of state and local party organizations.

The governor is automatically the president of both the University of California Board of Regents and the California State University Board of Trustees.

APPOINTMENT POWER

The governor has appointment power over departments and key policy makers. Several hundred of these appointments are for important board members and commissioners.

When a vacancy occurs due to death, removal or resignation, the governor makes appointments to fill the unexpired terms of:

. Statewide officers
. U.S. Senators
. Members of the U.S. House of Representatives
. County Supervisors
. Judicial vacancies, Municipal and Superior Courts
. State Supreme Court, Courts of Appeal Justices

JUDICIAL INFLUENCE

The governor has judicial influence through his or her power to nominate judges to the State Supreme Court, the Appeals Court and fill vacancies by appointment as they arise. With regards to convicted felons, the governor has the power to pardon, commute sentences and grant reprieves, but the reason for granting clemency must be reported to the legislature. *CLEMENCY is the governor's power to reduce or eliminate the sentences of convicted felons for humanitarian reasons.*

The governor may grant a ***PARDON**, which is the release of the convicted criminal from the legal consequences of the crime.* A governor may commute the sentence. ***COMMUTE** means a reduction in the length of a prison term.* A ***REPRIEVE** allows the governor to postpone a sentence of the court from being carried out.*

Without a doubt, the most controversial clemency power is the right of the governor to affect capital offenses. A ***CAPITAL PUNISHMENT** offense is one where the death penalty is prescribed by the court for the crime of taking, or involvement in the taking of, a human life and certain other serious crimes.*

COMMANDER-IN-CHIEF OF THE STATE MILITIA

The *COMMANDER-IN-CHIEF is the top official who directs the state militia (national guard).* The governor can call the national guard to active duty on his or her own initiative or upon the request of local officials in the event of a civil disturbance or natural disaster.

LEGISLATIVE LEADER

The legislative leadership is probably the most important power the governor possesses.

The governor is the ***LEGISLATIVE LEADER** of California, because he or she presents a personal agenda and annual budget to the legislature and can back up this leadership role with veto powers over legislation.*

The *STATE OF THE STATE ADDRESS is a speech by the governor, at the beginning of each legislative session in January, to inform the state senate and state assembly as to the condition of the state, his or her legislative agenda and recommendations for the year.* An annual state budget covering projected revenues and expenditures is prepared and submitted to the legislature. After the legislature passes its version of the budget back to the governor, the governor may reduce or eliminate particular budget items by use of the line item veto.

A revised budget bill is seldom signed "as is" by the governor. The *LINE ITEM VETO allows the governor to eliminate specific items and amounts from the proposed budget that are not to the governor's liking.* The biggest legislative weapon the governor holds is the full veto. A *VETO is the total rejection of any bill that can then only be overridden by a two-thirds vote of both the state assembly and senate, as opposed to a simple majority (51%).* A gubernatorial veto is difficult to override.

The constitutional revision of 1966 (extending time for legislative sessions) and the legislative re-organization of 1972 (continuous two-year session) effectively eliminated the pocket veto. A *POCKET VETO means that a governor fails to take any action on pending legislation after the legislature has adjourned.*

THE POWER TO MAKE LAWS

Bills that have been approved by both houses of the legislature are sent to the governor for his or her signature. The governor has 12 days after receiving the bill to do one of the following:

1) Sign the bill, thereby making it a law.
2) Not sign the bill, thereby making it law.
3) Veto the bill.

Remember: if two-thirds of both houses override the governor's veto, the bill becomes law.

Administration of the Executive Branch

There are many levels to the executive branch with thousands of people, making it resemble a giant corporation.

THE EXECUTIVE BRANCH APPOINTMENTS:

GOVERNOR'S CABINET
AGENCIES
DEPARTMENTS
DIVISIONS
* GOVERNOR'S PERSONAL STAFF
* Do not have to be confirmed by the senate

THE GOVERNOR'S CABINET

The *GOVERNOR'S CABINET is an advisory group that provides the chief executive with a comprehensive overview of state operations and has a hand in policy making and long-term planning for California.* Cabinet members are confirmed by the senate.

AGENCIES, DEPARTMENTS AND DIVISIONS

The administrators of these agencies are referred to as "secretaries of the agencies." The secretaries of the agencies provide leadership to the departments so that the governor can communicate efficiently between the numerous departments. The members of the governor's cabinet are usually secretaries of the agencies.

GOVERNOR'S PERSONAL STAFF

The *PERSONAL STAFF OF THE GOVERNOR is a group of approximately 100 coordinators who assist the governor in a variety of activities with the press, media, legislators, budget analysts and others.* Usually they were the governor's closest advisors when he or she was a private citizen. Unlike the governor's cabinet, the personal staff is not confirmed by the state senate.

California's Plural Executive

There are seven state elected officers, other than the governor and the four Board of Equalization members.

LIEUTENANT GOVERNOR

The *LIEUTENANT GOVERNOR is elected independently from the governor and, despite his or her title, has very few significant duties to perform in California.* The only official job of the lieutenant governor is to break a tie in the state senate; if such an event happens. The lieutenant governor is also an ex officio member of: the Board of Regents of the University of California, the Board of Trustees of the State University System, and the State Lands Commission, but these memberships take little time. The lieutenant governor has the powers of governor (state constitution) when the governor is incapacitated, out of the state or there is a vacancy.

ATTORNEY GENERAL

The *ATTORNEY GENERAL is director of the justice department in California and, as such, he or she is responsible for ensuring that the laws of the state are fairly enforced.* The attorney general is the most important executive officer in the state after the governor, acting as legal counsel for the state and most state agencies. The attorney general is responsible for the preparation of all ballot propositions submitted to the voters in state elections. The office is often a stepping-stone to governorship, for example: Earl Warren (1942); Edmund "Pat" Brown (1958); and George Deukmejian (1982).

STATE CONTROLLER

The *STATE CONTROLLER is chief accountant for the state.* The controller accounts for, and pays out, all state money. He or she advises local governments on financial matters and, in annual reports to the public, divulges their financial conditions. The controller chairs the Franchise Tax Board, which is

responsible for collection of state income taxes, and sits on the Board of Equalization, which collects the all-important state sales tax. He or she also chairs the State Lands Commission, and sits on the Water Resources Control Board. As you can see, the office of controller in the state of California is a very powerful one.

TREASURER

The ***TREASURER*** *is responsible for investing in bonds to fund large capital projects, such as construction of highways, schools and dams.* The treasurer has the responsibility of auctioning state bonds and, having custody of the state money, shifting state funds into banks and savings institutions that offer the highest interest rates. He or she must pool the various state accounts into a single high-yield investment program. The treasurer is responsible for deciding which financial underwriters are allowed to resell tax-exempt revenue bonds to investors.

SECRETARY OF STATE

The ***SECRETARY OF STATE*** *serves as the official record keeper of the acts of the legislature and the various executive departments and is the supervisor of all state elections.* He or she maintains the state archives and is the keeper of the Great Seal of California, which must be affixed to all documents signed by the governor. Businesses, counties and cities are granted incorporation charters by the secretary of state. Most importantly, the secretary of state must: enforce the state's election laws, print state ballot pamphlets, certify and publish election results, and check for the proper number of signatures on petitions for initiative, referendum and recall.

In addition, he or she must collect and approve statements of campaign donations and expenses. Many feel that the office of secretary of state should be nonpartisan because of the intense involvement in the conducting of elections and the approval of campaign contributions.

SUPERINTENDENT OF PUBLIC INSTRUCTION

The *SUPERINTENDENT OF PUBLIC INSTRUCTION is the director of the State Department of Education and is the only nonpartisan officer of the plural executive.* The department of education provides approximately 80% of the K-12 public school budget and sets standards for textbooks and curriculum. The superintendent is "Director of the Department of Education," but the policies for the department of education are established by the ten-member State Board of Education, all of whom are appointed by the governor. The superintendent is the secretary of the board and is supposed to implement the rules and regulations it adopts.

INSURANCE COMMISSIONER

The *INSURANCE COMMISSIONER is responsible for overseeing the massive California insurance industry, as a whole, and for the approval of all future auto insurance rate increases.* The office was changed from an appointed position to an elected one with the passage of Proposition 103 in 1988.

The insurance commissioner's position was created by the voters to reform auto insurance rates, which have been rising faster than food costs for some people. But the commissioner has already been faced with more comprehensive issues. Life insurance companies have failed because of an excessive reliance on junk bonds as an investment tool and our new state earthquake insurance program is already seriously under funded.

STATE BOARD OF EQUALIZATION

The *STATE BOARD OF EQUALIZATION is the five-member governmental body that is responsible for the assessment of all property in California.* The state is divided into 4 districts. An elected member from each district serves on the board along with the state controller, who serves ex officio. *EX OFFICIO means that the holder of one office (state controller) is automatically the holder of the second office (state board of equalization).*

The four board of equalization districts are:

District One. . . . . Northern California
District Two. . . . . Central California
District Three. . . . . Central Los Angeles Area
District Four . . . . South-Eastern California

The board of equalization is also responsible for collecting: 1) Sales Tax; 2) Cigarette Tax; 3) Gas Tax; 4) Alcohol Beverage Tax; and 5) Other Miscellaneous Taxes.

Recent Governors

The following five governors were elected for at least two terms and deserve special recognition.

Earl Warren "The Nonpartisan Advocate"
1943-1953 (three terms) Republican-Democrat

Earl Warren was so popular that he is the only governor in California history elected for three terms. He pushed for reforms in worker's compensation, prison conditions and old-age pensions but referred to them as progressive, not liberal, ideas. He was appointed Chief Justice of the U.S. Supreme Court by President Dwight D. Eisenhower in 1953 and later served as the head of the Warren Commission.

Edmund "Pat" Brown "The First Brown"
1959-1966 (two terms) Democrat

Edmund G. Brown faced controversy over the state problems of water development, smog control and capital punishment. By the end of his second term as governor, the state had greatly increased its spending. He more than doubled the miles of freeways, increased the State University and University of California Systems and began the huge State Water Project.

Ronald Reagan "The Conservative"
1967-1974 (two terms) Republican

Ronald Reagan, a conservative who did not like "big government spending," won the governorship easily. Although taxes and spending went up slightly while he was governor, he cut and trimmed the budget where he could. Reagan supported "law and order" but had trouble reforming welfare programs. His popularity carried him into the presidency of the United States for two terms.

Edmund "Jerry" Brown Jr. "The Non-traditionalist"
1975-1982 (two terms) Democrat

Jerry Brown was a non-traditional governor, interested in the quality of life. Brown, an environmentalist, wanted alternative energy sources. He was against Proposition 13, the property tax reduction initiative, but switched sides when he saw that the general public was behind it. That was the major factor in his landslide re-election in 1978.

George Deukmejian "The Uninteresting Conservative"
1983-1990 (two terms) Republican

"Duke," as the press called him, was a conservative who was mostly interested in keeping the cost of government down.

He took very seriously the responsibility of proposing a balanced budget. During his eight year tenure as governor, he used his veto authority 4,000 times because the legislature was consistently trying to spend more money than was available.

Pete Wilson "Growth Problem Handler"
1991- (two terms) Republican

Pete Wilson is a moderate Republican who seems to be on a mission to handle, or at least minimize, California's population growth problems. The challenge of increasing highway, school and prison construction, while trimming state funded services and increasing funding by raising taxes, will not win Wilson a popularity contest. But after decades of fiscal restraint, he

appears to be a real spender who is willing to tackle problems facing California.

Wilson believes California's growing pains must be solved or improved if we are to continue to accommodate the anticipated population growth and yet remain competitive. One of his priorities is keeping California companies from leaving the state.

California has a "plural" executive branch, meaning that less power is concentrated in the hands of a single chief executive. The governor works with eleven other elected officials, each running a separate part of the government. Unlike the governor's appointees and cabinet members, these plural executives will often represent different political parties than the governor. They include the lieutenant governor, attorney general, controller, secretary of state, treasurer, superintendent of public instruction, insurance commissioner and the four members of the board of equalization.

The governor of California has several important roles. He or she is the ceremonial leader of the state, greeting important dignitaries and representing California to the nation and the rest of the world. The governor is also the leader of his or her political party in California. He or she makes appointments to key state offices and commissions. The governor also nominates judges to the state supreme court, and fills vacancies on some of the lower courts. The governor has the power to grant clemency to convicted felons. The governor is automatically the commander-in-chief of the state militia, calling the national guard to active duty at will.

The governor's most important responsibility is that of legislative leader. The governor's office prepares a state budget and submits it to the legislature for approval. The legislature makes its adjustments and passes the budget back in the form of an appropriations bill. The governor then has the option of approving the budget, or reducing and eliminating specific budget items by using the "line item" veto power.

The governor has veto power over any bill passed by the legislature. It takes a two-thirds vote of both the assembly and the senate to override a gubernatorial veto. If the governor signs a bill, it becomes law.

The lieutenant governor has few significant duties. The attorney general is legal counsel for state and director of the justice department, responsible for the fair enforcement of California's laws. The state controller is the state's chief accountant and the chair of the Franchise Tax Board. The superintendent of public instruction, a nonpartisan post, directs the Department of Education. The secretary of state is California's official record-keeper, recording all acts of the legislature and overseeing elections. The state treasurer is responsible for supervising the bonds to finance huge public works projects. The insurance commissioner oversees the massive California insurance industry. The state board of equalization has four members plus the state controller. They are responsible for assessing real estate. They collect sales taxes and taxes on cigarettes, gasoline and alcohol.

1. Which plural executive has no assigned tasks and why?

2. What plural executive position was created by an initiative drive to cut the cost of owning an automobile?

3. How can the governor trim a budget bill without the help and cooperation of others?

4. Which of our recent governors served 2 or 3 terms?

5. Which one of our governors became Chief Justice of the Supreme Court? President of the United States?

CHAPTER 7 The California Legislature: Our Lawmakers

LEGISLATURE (OUR LAWMAKERS)

The California legislature, as the representative of the people, has the responsibility of making the laws and controlling the state's money. California has a bicameral legislature. ***BICAMERAL** is a legislature with two houses; in California it is made up of the state senate and assembly.* The state senate is referred to as the "upper house" and consists of only 40 members, whereas the state assembly, with 80 members, is called the "lower house."

How the State Legislature Functions

The main purpose of the legislature is to enact bills that:

1) **SPEND THE STATE'S MONEY**
2) **ESTABLISH STATE TAXES**
3) **MAKE STATE LAWS**

The legislature also has other functions such as: redistricting, placing constitutional amendments on the ballot, oversight responsibilities and the conducting of confirmation hearings.

LEGISLATIVE PROCESS

The legislature process in Sacramento begins with a bill. A *BILL is a draft of a law presented to the state senate or state assembly for approval or rejection.* Once a bill has been introduced by a member of one of the houses, it is sent to a legislative committee for study and revision. If it gains committee approval, the bill is sent to the floor of that house for a vote by the entire membership. Eventually, a majority in each house must agree on the bill before it is sent to the governor.

BILLS NEXT GO TO THE GOVERNOR

The governor, after receiving a bill, has 12 days in which to sign, not sign or veto it. If the governor signs or does not take any action on the bill, it becomes law. If the governor vetoes the bill it is dead, unless two-thirds of the members in each house vote to override the veto.

THE LEGISLATURE MAY OVERRIDE A VETO

The legislature may override the governor's veto. A *VETO OVERRIDE means that the legislature can make laws, even if the governor vetoes a bill, by obtaining the required two-thirds vote of the members in each house.* In recent history, Governor Edmund "Jerry" Brown Jr. (1975-1982) vetoed about 10% of all bills sent to him, causing a large number of veto overrides.

LEGISLATIVE SESSIONS

The legislature meets in time periods referred to as sessions. The *GENERAL SESSION is a two-year period that starts at noon on the first Monday in December, during even-numbered years, and ends on November 30th of the next even-numbered year.* Legislators have become year-round professionals: For good or bad the legislature seems to be a full-time career. This may change now with the passage of the term limitation initiative that limits the careers of all state elected officials to two terms (8 years total) for state senators and three terms (6 years total) for assembly members.

THE FUNCTIONS OF THE CALIFORNIA STATE LEGISLATURE

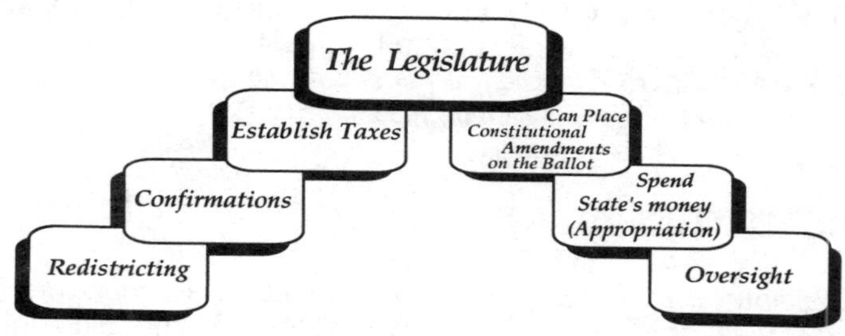

The Major Functions of the California State Legislature

BUDGET BILL

Each year before January 11th, the governor must submit his or her proposed budget for consideration to the senate and assembly. The budget bill must be enacted in both houses by midnight, on June 15th, annually. This deadline has not always been met in the past.

A *SPECIAL SESSION can be called by the governor to deal with urgent matters.* Legislative action is limited to only the subject specified by the governor.

REAPPORTIONMENT (REDISTRICTING)

REAPPORTIONMENT is the process of dividing districts into groups that are approximately equal in population. This process is also called re-mapping, mapping, redistricting or districting. The principle of equal-elective representation requires districts to be redrawn at the beginning of each decade to conform to changes in population.

The legislature reapportions not only the state assembly, but the U.S. congressional and board of equalization districts.

The problem with having legislators do the reapportioning is that the majority party will naturally draw the district lines so that it will have the voter support advantage in elections. ***GERRYMANDERING*** *is the process of redrawing district lines to increase the number of seats held by the majority party.*

CONSTITUTIONAL AMENDMENT

The legislature, by the passage of a constitutional amendment in 1962, was provided with a new method of amending the state constitution. If two-thirds of the membership of each house concur, the legislature can submit a constitutional amendment directly to the people by simply placing it on the ballot where it must then be ratified by a majority of the voters.

OVERSIGHT

Certain committees in the legislature perform an oversight function. ***OVERSIGHT COMMITTEES*** *act as watchdogs to make sure legislation, or programs that have been passed by the legislature, are being carried out properly by the employees of the executive branch. They also review the efficiency of programs to see if these programs can be accomplished more economically.*

When an oversight committee's investigation reveals a severe case of impropriety, the state constitution allows the legislature to proceed with impeachment. ***IMPEACHMENT*** *is the process by which the legislature formally charges an elected official with misconduct.* The assembly must first vote for the articles of impeachment before they can be sent to the senate. The elected official is then tried in the senate where a two-thirds vote of the full membership is necessary to remove the official.

This severe measure, however, is rare. In general, oversight is not as exciting or glamorous for legislators as introducing bills or handling constituency problems, but it is a vital function of a bureaucracy in order to help make for an effective and efficient government.

CONFIRMATIONS

CONFIRMATION is the process in the state senate of either approving or rejecting, by a majority vote, the hundreds of appointments made by the governor. Confirmation hearings are held for the heads of the governor's cabinet, commissions, boards and even the director of the department of motor vehicles. The senate rules committee holds hearings on the fitness of all the nominees and makes a recommendation to the full membership of the senate. If the full senate approves a candidate by a simple majority vote, the candidate is confirmed. The assembly does not play an active role in the confirmation process, although the candidate does need a two-thirds approval vote from the assembly as well as the senate.

California Senate

CALIFORNIA SENATE (UPPER HOUSE)

The *CALIFORNIA SENATE is the upper house in the legislature with 40 members serving 4 year-terms (2 term limit), with half of the senate districts conducting elections every 2 years.* The U.S. Supreme Court now requires the upper house of a state legislature to be based on population rather than the geographic size of the county. This has resulted in a shift of more senate seats to Southern California.

The senate has, for many years, been more stable, less partisan and more conservative in its procedures than the assembly. Each senator represents over 750,000 people. The number of senators has been set by the state constitution at 40, exactly half the size of the state assembly.

SENATE LEADERSHIP

According to our state constitution, the *LIEUTENANT GOVERNOR is automatically the president of the senate but, in actuality, this is largely a ceremonial post.* He or she has no role of note in senate matters unless there is a rare 20-20 vote; then the lieutenant governor provides the tie-breaking vote.

The powerful *SENATE PRESIDENT PRO TEMPORE is the member elected by the senate to be its leader.* Since the lieutenant governor is rarely present during most sessions, the actual leadership of the upper house is vested in the senate president pro tempore. Chosen by fellow senators, the "pro tem" is the one who presides over the senate.

The *SENATE RULES COMMITTEE is chaired by the senate president pro tempore, and includes four other members elected by the senate.* This committee has the power to appoint all the other senate committee chairs and vice-chairs. The senate rules committee is also extremely powerful in that it decides which committee will be assigned to each bill coming up for consideration. It also selects the senators who will serve on executive and judicial boards and commissions.

The *MAJORITY AND MINORITY FLOOR LEADERS are senate members appointed by their party to direct the party's political strategy in the legislature.*

THE PRESTIGE OF THE SENATE

The senate chamber is decorated in deep reds, the tradition of the upper class—and with good reason. The "upper house," with its small number of representatives and long term, is more select—and, therefore, more prestigious—than the assembly. If an assembly member has a chance to win election to the senate, he or she will usually do so. But now that we have term limitations, don't be surprised if you see senate members switch to the assembly—and visa-versa—just to remain in the legislature for a few more terms.

California Assembly

THE CALIFORNIA ASSEMBLY (LOWER HOUSE)

The *CALIFORNIA STATE ASSEMBLY is the lower house in the legislature with 80 members serving two-year terms (3 term limit).* The assembly is known for its power struggles and is generally more volatile than the senate.

Requirements for Legislators

ELIGIBILITY... At least 18 years of age.

RESIDENCY... California resident for three years, at least one year in the district (immediately prior).

TERM LIMIT... Two, four-year terms for the senate (8 years) and three, two-year terms (6 years) for the assembly.

SENATE SEAT ROTATION... 20 seats each even-numbered year.

ASSEMBLY SEAT ROTATION... All 80 seats even-numbered years.

BOTH HOUSES... Bound by the code of ethics—may expel a member by two-thirds vote.

COMPENSATION... $52,500 salary and $92 per day living expenses when in session. Telephone and gasoline expense allowance for a state licensed automobile. Limited health and retirement benefits.

ASSEMBLY LEADERSHIP

The powerful *SPEAKER OF THE ASSEMBLY is the presiding officer of the assembly, elected by the membership and automatically serving (ex officio) on all assembly and joint legislative committees.* His or her powers parallel those of the president pro tempore, the counterpart in the senate. The speaker names a member of his or her political party to be the majority floor leader. But the entire assembly elects an *ASSEMBLY SPEAKER PRO TEMPORE who actually runs the proceedings during the speaker's absence.* The speaker also chairs the assembly's rules committee. This important position allows the speaker to control the flow of legislative activity on the floor—in much the same way that the senate's rules committee chair (the pro tem) controls the legislative business of that house.

The *MAJORITY PARTY FLOOR LEADER is appointed by the speaker to represent the majority party.* The *MINORITY FLOOR LEADER is chosen by, and represents, the minority party.* The minority floor leader is also called the "minority whip."

Committee System

The legislature does all of its work by the use of the committee system. A *COMMITTEE SYSTEM is a system whereby the legislature is broken down into committees; a basic working component that can study all bills in depth.* Most new bills are first referred to one of the standing committees for in-depth study and review.

THE DIFFERENT TYPES OF COMMITTEES

The *RULES COMMITTEES are powerful committees that refer all bills to standing committees, as well as selecting and supervising the assembly and senate support staffs.* It is chaired, in the senate, by the pro tem and in the assembly by the speaker.

STANDING COMMITTEES are the basic, or core, committees that will do most of the work for the current session and are established by the rules of each house at the beginning of each session. There are currently 30 established standing committees in the assembly and 23 in the senate. Good old-fashioned politics determines who controls these committees and what the exact membership will be during each session. Each committee is assigned bills, according to its jurisdiction, which it will hear, study, hold public hearings on, change as needed and finally vote on in committee.

STANDING COMMITTEES:

Agriculture and Water Resources
Appropriations
Banking, Commerce, Trade
Budget and Fiscal Review
Business and Professions
Constitutional Amendments
Education
Elections and Reapportionment
Energy and Public Utilities
Governmental Organization
Health and Human Services
Housing and Urban Affairs
Industrial Relations
Insurance & Corporations
Judiciary
Local Government
Natural Resources and Wildlife
Public Employment / Retirement
Revenue and Taxation Rules
Toxic / Public Safety Management
Transportation
Veterans Affairs

In addition to the standing committees in each house, the legislature also employs joint committees. *JOINT COMMITTEES are committees consisting of an equal number of assembly members and senators who study subjects of mutual interest to both houses.* They recommend legislation that they believe will be acceptable to both houses.

FISCAL COMMITTEES are standing financial committees that oversee the annual state budget and handle all other bills that either directly or indirectly involve a cost to the state.

CONFERENCE COMMITTEES are set up to resolve differences between the assembly and the senate versions of the same bill.

SELECT OR SPECIAL COMMITTEES are set up by either house to research limited subject areas where the forming of a permanent standing committee may not be seen as necessary.

Proposition 140

Term Limitations ...

Proposition 140, although called the term limitation initiative, actually does three things:

1) Limits the terms of state senators to two (8 total years). Limits the terms of assembly members to three (6 total years). Limits the terms of governor and other state elected officials to two (8 total years).

2) Eliminates the state legislative pension system.

3) Mandates a 38% cut in the legislator's office budget forcing massive staff reductions (most have been restored).

Californians see term limitations for officeholders as a first step in making the political process more responsive to new people, new programs and change!

LEGISLATORS SALARY AND BENEFITS

Both chambers of the California legislature receive the same base salary of $52,500 a year and, when the legislature is in session, a $92 daily living expense allowance (per diem). The assembly speaker and the senate president pro tempore each receive a salary of $63,000. All legislators receive round-trip travel expenses to and from legislative sessions and committee meetings, gas and telephone credit cards and use of a state-licensed auto. The salary package formerly included generous health and retirement benefits.

Types of Legislation

(BILLS AND RESOLUTIONS)

There are basically two types of legislation: bills and resolutions. The most important type, as discussed earlier, is a bill. Most of the work done by the legislature is expressed in the form of bills. The state budget and state taxes are no exception; new budgets and taxes are discussed, revised, and approved or rejected as bills. The majority of California's bills pass through the legislature according to the procedure described in "Legislative Process." Two special kinds of bills, however, follow different rules.

An ***APPROPRIATION BILL*** *is one that authorizes funds to be spent from state revenues.* ***URGENT BILLS*** *are bills that must take effect immediately after being enacted.* These two types of bills require a two-thirds approval of each house.

Bills are assigned numbers so that they can be identified easily. Assembly bills have an (AB) before each number and (SB) is placed before a senate bill.

The second type of legislation is the resolution. A ***RESOLUTION*** *is a vote on a matter that involves one house, or in some instances both the assembly and senate, but does not require the governor's approval.* There are four kinds of resolutions:

CONSTITUTIONAL AMENDMENT - known as ACA or SCA depending on the house of origination. A constitutional amendment is a resolution to change our state's constitution. An amendment must pass by a two-thirds majority in each house before it can be placed on the next election ballot. It must be ratified by a majority of those voting before the constitution can be changed.

CONCURRENT RESOLUTION - known as ACR or SCR depending on the house of origination. This is used to adopt joint rules, establish joint committees and congratulate groups or individuals. A simple majority of each house is needed to pass a concurrent resolution.

JOINT RESOLUTION - known as AJR or SJR depending on where it originated. This action urges the U.S. congress to pass or defeat legislation currently before it. In this way the state legislature lets its opinion be known regarding national issues.

HOUSE RESOLUTION - known as AR or SR depending on the house of origination. A house resolution is used to create one-term committees, amend rules of that house and congratulate groups and individuals. These resolutions are usually adopted by a voice vote of the majority.

TRACKING LEGISLATION (BILLS)

A person can receive a free copy of a current bill, as it goes through the legislature, by simply going to the "bill room" in the basement of the state capital building in Sacramento.

With the huge number of bills introduced in each two-year legislative session, both houses publish guides to help keep interested people informed. The *DAILY FILE is an agenda of that day's business,* whereas the *DAILY JOURNAL contains an account of the preceding day.*

In addition to these guides, histories are published by each house. There is *DAILY HISTORY, WEEKLY HISTORY, SEMIFINAL HISTORY, A FINAL HISTORY and a LEGISLATIVE INDEX of the entire two-year legislative session. These all summarize the actions taken on bills during this period.*

Legislative Staff

EMPLOYEES

The legislature of California has one of the largest staffs in the United States. Each legislative member is entitled to an administrative assistant and secretaries for both his or her capital office and also the district office.

JOINT STAFF

The *LEGISLATIVE COUNSEL is the chief legal counsel for the legislature and is selected at the beginning of each session by the agreement of both houses.* Most bills are prepared by the legislative counsel's office. This counsel advises the legislature on the legality and constitutionality of measures and prepares indexes of the California codes and statutes.

The *LEGISLATIVE ANALYST provides the legislature with financial, economic and fiscal advice. He or she is appointed by the joint legislative budget committee.* The staff of the legislative analyst's office evaluates every item in the proposed state budget and all bills (appropriation bills) requiring money that go before the fiscal (revenue and expenditure) committee. Most important to the general public is the fact that the legislative analyst prepares a financial analysis of each proposition to be included in the state ballot pamphlet.

The *AUDITOR GENERAL is appointed by the joint legislative audit committee to assist the legislature by examining, auditing and reporting on the financial statements submitted by the executive branch.*

Media Coverage

CAL-SPAN

In 1991, after months of tests and dress rehearsals, the California assembly (lower house) started to televise its proceedings live on cable television. *CAL-SPAN is the nonprofit company that distributes the signal to a statewide cable system that is available to over two million subscribers.*

NEWSPAPERS AND SERVICES

ASSOCIATED PRESS
BAKERSFIELD CALIFORNIAN
CAPITOL NEWS SERVICE
CONTRA COSTA TIMES
COPLEY NEWS SERVICE
DAILY RECORDER
GANNETT NEWS SERVICE
LONG BEACH/
PRESS TELEGRAM
LOS ANGELES DAILY JOURNAL
LOS ANGELES DAILY NEWS
LOS ANGELES TIMES
OAKLAND TRIBUNE
ORANGE COUNTY REGISTER
RIVERSIDE PRESS
SACRAMENTO BEE
SAN DIEGO TRIBUNE
SAN DIEGO UNION
SAN FRANCISCO CHRONICLE
SAN FRANCISCO EXAMINER
SAN JOSE MERCURY NEWS
UNITED PRESS INTERNATIONAL

MAGAZINES

CALIFORNIA JOURNAL
GOLDEN STATE REPORT

NEWSLETTERS

CALIFORNIA EYE / THE
POLITICAL ANIMAL
CALIFORNIA POLITICAL WEEK
POLITICAL PULSE
NEW WEST NOTES

C-SPAN—NATIONAL COVERAGE

C-SPAN, the nation's television programmer for the federal government, is very successful. It is so successful that it broadcasts "full-time coverage" of all types of events that are affected by federal policy. Its reports are entirely objective and nonpartisan.

NEWSPAPERS AND NEWS SERVICES

Californians are kept up-to-date on political news from Sacramento by reading newspapers and periodicals, listening to the radio and watching network programming or cable coverage. Since Sacramento, the capital, is the political news center, many newspapers, news services, magazines and newsletters have capital bureaus stationed there.

Chapter Summary

The California state legislature is patterned after the national legislature in Washington, D.C.. It is a "bicameral" legislature in that it consists of two houses; the state senate and the state assembly. The senate (or upper house) has forty members. The assembly (or lower house) has eighty. Bills are drafts of proposed legislative action. They are used by the legislature to create new laws, approve the spending of money or to permit the legislature to raise money through taxes. A bill must be approved by a majority of both houses before it can be passed on to the governor for approval. Certain bills and resolutions (such as appropriations bills, urgent bills and constitutional amendments) require a two-thirds majority vote in each house to be approved. Resolutions are legislative votes on matters that do not require the governor's approval.

Senate members serve four-year terms and assembly members serve two-year terms. Under term limitations (Prop. 140), senators may serve for eight years (two terms) while assembly members serve for no more than six years (three terms). To hold a legislative seat, a person must be at least 18 years old and be a California resident for at least three years (living in the represented district for at least one year).

With only forty members, the state senate (or upper house) is more prestigious than the assembly. Each senator represents more than 750,000 citizens. The lieutenant governor is the ceremonial president of the senate, but the real leader is the senate president pro tempore. The pro tem is elected by the senate and is the counterpart to the speaker of the assembly. He or she controls the flow of legislation, makes important committee appointments and chairs the powerful senate rules committee (comparable to the rules committee in the assembly). The pro tem controls the purse strings of the state, since the rules committee must approve all expenditures. Each party also appoints a majority or minority floor leader.

The presiding officer of the assembly is the speaker. The speaker is elected, and serves on all joint legislative committees. This very powerful position dominates the legislature, controlling the flow of legislative activity, controlling the size and membership of all the committees and appointing committee chairs and other important posts. The speaker appoints the majority party floor leader to represent his or her party during the session. The minority party also has its own floor leader. A speaker pro tempore (or pro tem) is selected by the membership to run the day-to-day proceedings. The pro tem is an automatic member of the powerful assembly rules committee, but has no vote. The assembly rules committee is chaired by the speaker. It controls the flow of all bills through the assembly and also supervises the assembly support staff.

Each legislative session lasts two years, starting the first Monday in December on even numbered years and ending two years later on November 30th. Every year the governor must submit a proposed budget by January 11th. The legislature is required to work with the governor's budget and both houses must enact it by June 15th. The governor calls a "special session" of the legislature to deal with a specific urgent matter.

Another difficult responsibility for the state legislature (political gamesmanship) is reapportionment, or re-mapping, of the state assembly and the U.S. congressional districts.

1. What does the state legislature do for us?

2. Why does a senator have "more prestige?"

3. Why do the assembly speaker and the senate president pro tempore have so much power?

4. What is the difference between a bill and a resolution?

5. Term limitations had what effect on the legislators?

THE GREAT SEAL OF THE STATE OF
HE MIND

CHAPTER 8 Our Judicial System

Most Californians have little direct contact with the state's judicial system except for the occasional traffic ticket, but this system of courts, commissions, and agencies is an essential part of our government.

JUSTICE IS PRIMARILY A "STATE ACTIVITY"

The *CALIFORNIA JUDICIAL SYSTEM is the branch of the state government whose job is to administer justice under the law.* Unlike many other government operations, the judicial system is run primarily by the state. Only federal law violations and appeals of California Supreme Court decisions can be heard in federal courts. Ninety percent of all court cases filed in California are handled by our state courts.

Our California judicial system, as a whole, is considered one of the most progressive in the nation. It consists not only of our courts, but of a network of agencies and departments working together. This network—representing not just the judicial branch, but the executive and legislative branches as well—includes the groups listed in the following chart:

1. Four-Level Court Structure
2. Commissions and the Judicial Council
3. Attorneys and the State Bar
4. Peace Officers
5. Participating Citizens
6. Correction and Rehabilitation

California's Four-Level Court Structure

Article VI of the California Constitution of 1879 declared that judicial power to legally interpret justice lies in our four California courts, listed here in descending order:

. California Supreme Court
. California Courts of Appeal
. Superior Court (lawsuits over $25,000)
. Municipal Court (lawsuits $25,000 and under)

Both criminal and civil cases are heard by all four of the basic courts in California. A *CRIMINAL CASE involves a serious breach of the public law. CIVIL CASES are brought against private parties by private parties, usually for business or financial reasons.*

MUNICIPAL COURTS

The lower courts in California are called municipal courts. A *MUNICIPAL COURT is the lower court for criminal and civil actions.* Municipal courts have original jurisdiction in most civil cases where the amount in question is $25,000 or less. All sudden vacancies and new positions are filled by the governor, but most municipal court justices are elected to six-year terms.

SMALL CLAIMS COURTS are municipal courts for civil cases where the current maximum judgment for the prevailing party is $5,000. A *JUDGMENT is the amount of money awarded for damages by the judge to the winner in a court case.* (In a jury trial, the jury decides the amount of judgment.) Neither party is allowed to be represented in the courtroom by an attorney.

The *PLAINTIFF is the party filing the civil action in court or the state filing a case in a criminal action.* The *DEFENDANT is the person being sued or being charged with a crime.*

SUPERIOR COURTS

At least one *SUPERIOR COURT is located in each county; it is the state's basic civil and criminal trial court for cases involving damages in excess of $25,000.* The court's case load is made up mainly of:

. Civil cases and personal injury cases over $25,000
. Marital dissolution
. Guardianship petitions
. Probate of estates

Only about 25% of the cases are criminal cases—which must carry a possible jail term of a year or more—or juvenile delinquency problems.

COURTS: EITHER TRIAL OR APPELLATE COURTS

The four-tier court system can be divided into two main types of courts: trial and appellate. A *TRIAL COURT is a local court where the facts are determined and a decision is made by a judge (or jury, if requested).* Municipal and superior courts are generally considered to be trial courts, but can also serve as appellate courts. An *APPELLATE COURT determines whether the proper procedures were used in the original trial and whether the law was properly applied or interpreted.* Normally the state supreme court and the courts of appeal only hear cases on appeal.

COURTS OF APPEAL

The *COURTS OF APPEAL are set up to hear appeals from lower courts and relieve the case load on the California supreme court.*

Like the supreme court, they only hear cases that deal with the legal interpretation of a lower court decision. There are six district courts of appeal.

THE CALIFORNIA SUPREME COURT

The *CALIFORNIA SUPREME COURT is made up of seven justices—the chief justice and six associate justices—and is the highest court in the state.* A decision from this court is binding on

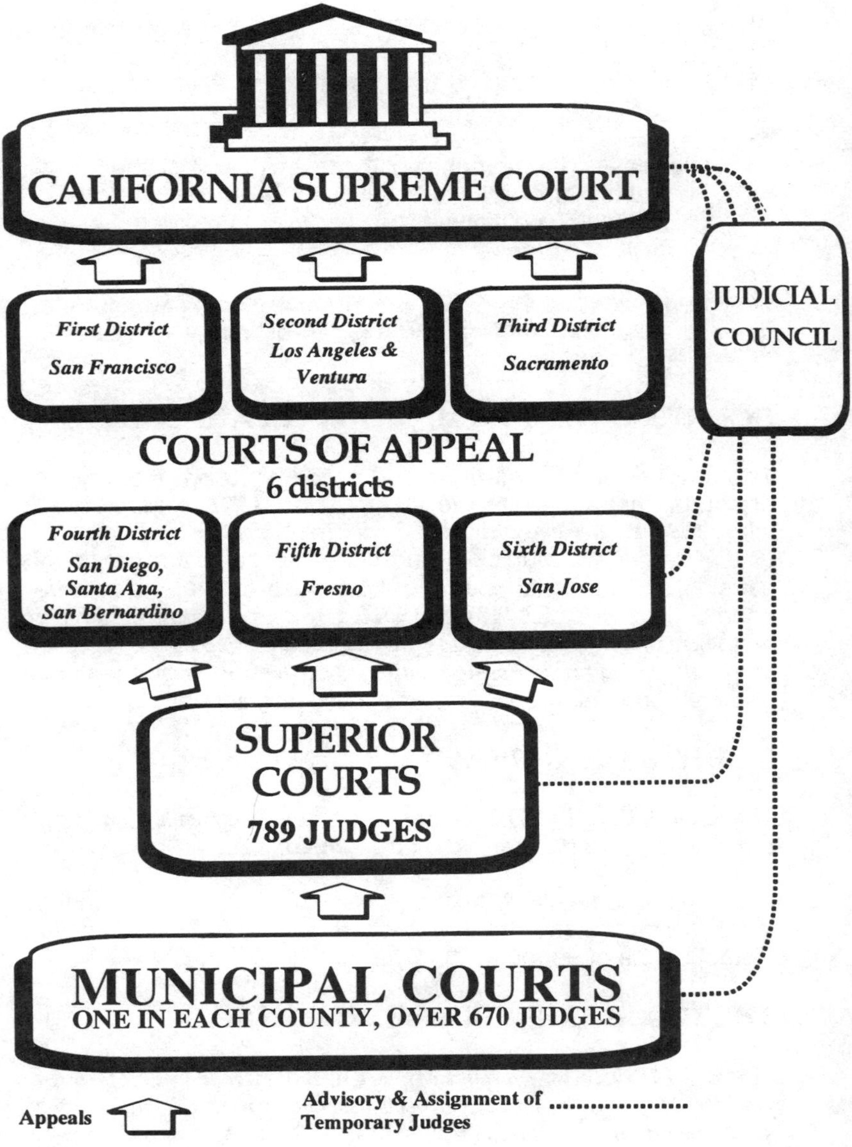

CALIFORNIA SUPREME COURT
First District
San Francisco
Second District
Los Angeles &
Ventura
Third District
Sacramento
JUDICIAL
COUNCIL
COURTS OF APPEAL
6 districts
Fourth District
San Diego,
Santa Ana,
San Bernardino
Fifth District
Fresno
Sixth District
San Jose
SUPERIOR
COURTS
789 JUDGES
MUNICIPAL COURTS
ONE IN EACH COUNTY, OVER 670 JUDGES
Appeals
Advisory & Assignment of
Temporary Judges

all the other courts in California. All death-row cases are automatically appealed to the supreme court. If the state supreme court so desires, it can remove a case from a lower court and hear it directly. This is only done when the court wants to rule on a matter or subject quickly.

JUSTICES FACE ELECTION AFTER APPOINTMENT

After the justices of the state supreme court and the state courts of appeal are appointed by the governor, they must first be confirmed by the commission on judicial appointments and then be voted on by the public at the next gubernatorial election. If the voters approve the governor's appointment, the justice continues in that position for a 12-year term after which he or she can once again run for another 12-year term. In addition, all superior and municipal court judges, if appointed to fill emergency vacancies, must run for the balance of their term at the next regularly scheduled gubernatorial election. They must then run for re-election at the end of each term.

In an effort to keep political bias out of our courts, all judges in California are elected on a nonpartisan ballot.

Commissions and the Judicial Council

Our state judicial system has three commissions and one council that protect the integrity and efficiency of California's court system. They are the:

1. Commission on Judicial Appointments (Courts of Appeal and Supreme Court)
2. Commission on Judicial Nominees (Evaluation of nominees for all the other courts)
3. Commission on Judicial Performance (Ethics)
4. Judicial Council (Keeping courts efficient)

CONFIRMATION: HIGHER COURT JUSTICES

The *COMMISSION ON JUDICIAL APPOINTMENTS consists of three members who must confirm all judicial nominees for the California courts of appeal and supreme court.* The three members of the commission on judicial appointments are as follows: the chief justice of the state supreme court, the attorney general of California and a senior presiding justice of a district court of appeals. Their job is to hold hearings where law enforcement officials, members of the state bar and private citizens can express their opinions or concerns about the chosen nominee.

NOMINATIONS: LOWER COURT JUSTICES

The *COMMISSION ON JUDICIAL NOMINEES is a 25-member commission appointed by the Board of Governors of the State Bar of California (a private association of attorneys) to recommend nominees to the governor for appointment to the bench, except for those nominated for courts of appeal or supreme court positions.* The governor can appoint any nominee he or she desires, but traditionally will not oppose the commission's recommendations.

COMMISSION ON JUDICIAL PERFORMANCE

The *COMMISSION ON JUDICIAL PERFORMANCE is a commission of nine private citizens that acts as a monitor (watchdog) of judges and their conduct in and out of the courtroom.* The commission on judicial performance can recommend forced retirement or removal of any judge.

THE JUDICIAL COUNCIL

The *JUDICIAL COUNCIL is a hard-working group that has the responsibility of improving the fairness and efficiency of our entire state court system.* The council oversees the business operations of our state courts and reports its recommendations for improvement to the legislature and the governor. It attempts to provide alternatives to litigation and reduce the cost and complexity of court proceedings. In addition, the council addresses issues of racism, sexism, and language bias (against non-English speakers) in the courts. But most importantly, it plans for the future of the court system and its sources of funding.

REMOVING AN UNWANTED JUDGE

In California there are four ways to remove a judge:

1. Through the normal election process.
2. Impeachment and conviction by the state legislature.
3. By recall election—called if 20% of the registered voters sign a recall petition.
4. If convicted of a felony or moral turpitude—must be recommended by commission on judicial performance.

CALIFORNIA AND THE U.S. SUPREME COURT

Usually, the U.S. supreme court will only hear a case litigated in a lower federal court or in a state court if it involves an issue of federal law. The U.S. supreme court also determines whether a state constitution or state law conforms to the allowed provisions of the federal constitution. The state courts are bound by its decisions. In most states, cases must go through the state supreme court before being passed on to the U.S. supreme court. In California, however, cases may also go to the U.S. supreme court directly from a California court of appeals.

Court Procedures

CRIMINAL CASES

After being arrested, the accused is brought before a judge, usually a municipal court judge, to be arraigned. An *ARRAIGNMENT is the court session where the judge officially informs accused parties of their legal rights and the charges against them.* The judge sets the date of the preliminary hearing and determines bail. *BAIL is the amount of money that must be posted before a person can be released from jail.* If the accused is of little danger to the public, he or she can be released without bail, or, *"on his or her OWN RECOGNIZANCE."*

"3-strikes"

Increases sentences for convicted felons who have previous convictions for certain serious or violent felonies. Includes as prior convictions certain felonies committed by older juveniles. Fiscal impact: Reaffirms existing law, which results in annual state costs initially of hundreds of millions increasing to billions of dollars. Unknown net impact on local governments. Unknown state and local savings for costs of crimes not committed. Here's how it works:

Strike One: One serious/violent felony serves as a first strike toward a stiffer prison term.

Strike Two: A second felony conviction, with one prior serious-violent felony, DOUBLES the base sentence for the conviction. No probation.

Strike three: A third felony conviction, with two serious-violent prior felonies, TRIPLES the base sentence or imposes 25 years to life, whichever is greater. No probation.

Some people say that this law is bad because nonviolent offenders are lumped together with violent criminals and the cost to the entire legal system will be huge, especially as the prisoners age.

Most criminal cases are resolved without a trial. Since trials are costly and time-consuming, the courts encourage plea bargaining instead. ***PLEA BARGAINING** is a negotiated agreement between the prosecutor and the defense attorney to accept a plea of guilty to a lesser crime than the defendant was originally accused of.* Although our court system would be overwhelmed if every defendant decided to have a jury trial, some people believe that plea bargaining is "soft" on criminals and should be avoided.

State Supreme Court ... Discards Its Activist Role

The California supreme court is now dominated by conservatives who are less willing than previous justices to expand the people's rights beyond the scope of the state constitution. Under Chief Justice Malcolm Lucas, the court is not actively seeking to extend state constitutional protections.

How they rule in the next several years will determine the exact label to be given this court. The state supreme court will be ruling on some of the following questions:

1. Should graduation prayer be permitted?
2. Can the state lend textbooks to religious schools?
3. Do unmarried minors need their parents' consent for an abortion?
4. Can unequal funds be spent on different classes of students in certain schools?

In order to establish clear guidelines for punishment, crimes have been grouped into three major categories: infractions, misdemeanors, and felonies. ***INFRACTIONS** are the least serious types of crimes, such as traffic violations.* The punishment for an infraction is usually a fine and, in rare cases, jail time. ***MISDEMEANORS** are more serious crimes, including such acts as drunk driving or shoplifting.* Misdemeanor convictions carry fines and jail time of less than one year in prison. ***FELONIES** are the most serious types of crimes and include such crimes as grand theft auto, drug trafficking and murder.* These crimes are punishable by prison terms of over a year and, under special circumstances, even death.

An alternative to prison terms is probation. ***PROBATION** is the act of suspending the sentence of a convicted offender and giving the offender supervised freedom.*

CIVIL CASES

In a civil case the court procedure is much simpler. The plaintiff files a complaint with the court clerk. A *COMPLAINT is the legal charge or charges brought against the defendant.* The court then issues a subpoena (or summons) for the defendant and hears both sides of the case. If the court finds in favor of the plaintiff, "punishment" of the defendant might include, for example, paying damages or surrendering custody of a child—not prison time.

JUVENILE OFFENDERS

JUVENILES are people under the age of 18 and, because of this fact, are treated differently from adults in our legal system.

Our society wants to protect the juvenile and itself at the same time. A juvenile is not sent to jail or prison, but rather to juvenile hall until his or her case is heard and, if convicted, will be sent to a detention center where society will try to rehabilitate that person.

Attorneys and the State Bar

CITIZENS' RIGHT TO AN ATTORNEY

The California constitution and the U.S. constitution both provide that a person accused of a crime has the right to be represented by an attorney.

STATE BAR ASSOCIATION

No person can practice law without first being admitted to the state bar. The *STATE BAR OF CALIFORNIA is the professional organization that is authorized by the state constitution to admit candidates to practice law in California, set ethical standards, and discipline and expel attorneys.*

PROSECUTING AND DEFENSE ATTORNE

The ***DISTRICT ATTORNEY (D.A.)*** *is the prosecuting attorne for the government at the county level.* He or she evaluates the cases brought before the D.A.'s office and decides which cases should go to trial.

As discussed earlier, few criminal cases actually go to trial. The cost to the judicial system would be astronomical if every criminal case did. In most instances the district attorney will drop up to half of all felony charges and only prosecute the solid cases where there is good, factual evidence.

The ***DEFENSE ATTORNEY*** *is the attorney for the defendant.* A ***PUBLIC DEFENDER*** *is a county-employed attorney who has the job of defending the accused person, in a criminal case, when the defendant cannot afford an attorney.* Legal services for the indigent are also offered by such groups as Legal Aid.

Peace Officers

A ***POLICE OFFICER*** *is employed by a city and sworn to uphold justice.* The bulk of law enforcement work by the police is carried out at the street level. City police chiefs are usually appointed by the city manager or the police commission. The police officer's counterpart in the unincorporated county areas is called a sheriff's deputy.

A ***SHERIFF*** *is a peace officer who works for the county, runs the county jail and provides a crime lab for the city police within that county if needed.* The county sheriff, the top administrative officer, is elected through a nonpartisan election.

A ***HIGHWAY PATROL OFFICER*** *is a state peace officer who protects our safety on highways and state or county roads.*

The job of the ***STATE POLICE*** *is to protect state buildings, the governor and other state officials.*

ION & TATION

)0,000 convicts in prison and about California Youth Authority system. The inmat on is now increasing at the rate of over 10,000 per year. The cost to the public for housing all the inmates in California is over $2.1 billion a year and climbing. How will California deal with this problem?

Reformers say there must be a better and cheaper way, while hard-liners feel that we are not strict enough and want even stiffer penalties for certain crimes.

The cost of keeping a prisoner in jail for a year is $20,000. Hard-liners would argue that these same people would cost society more than that amount if they were left on the streets to continue their crimes.

About 3.5% of our population is in a state prison. What a waste! Worse yet, according to prison officials, by the year 2000 California's inmate population will exceed 200,000. We will have to do more than just build our way out of the prison crisis.

A ***MARSHAL** is a county peace officer who runs the courtrooms, serves court-related legal papers and physically evicts tenants if ordered.* His or her main job is to protect the judges.

Citizens' Participation

Citizens can participate in the judicial system as witnesses, jury members, or grand jury members.

***A WITNESS** is an individual who has seen something relevant to the commission of a crime.*

In a ***JURY TRIAL,*** *a group of 12 men and women (or less) judges whether the accused is innocent or guilty of the charges.* In civil trials, the number of jurors is reduced to eight in order to hold down court costs. Jury members are selected from the county voter registration roll and DMV records.

Every county has a grand jury. A ***GRAND JURY*** *is a group of 19 citizens (23 in Los Angeles) who investigate criminal activity and county government and issue reports to the public.* The grand jury, selected by the county's superior court judges, serves for a period of one year and acts as the county's "watchdog." At the end of that year, it must submit a final report to the county board of supervisors. The grand jury has the power, in unusual cases, to indict someone. An ***INDICTMENT*** *is a complaint against a person, charging that person with a crime.*

Our judicial system is primarily a state, not federal, entity. It is a network of courts, agencies, and other groups including police departments, the state bar, and the prison and parole systems.

The California court system has four levels: The lowest courts are the municipal courts. These courts have original jurisdiction in most civil cases where the amount in question is under $25,000. Small claims courts are a type of lower court specializing in simple civil cases where the amount is currently $5,000 or less.

The next level up in the court system is the superior court. Superior courts specialize in civil cases that involve amounts in excess of $25,000 and also handle divorce proceedings, guardianship petitions, probates, and some serious criminal and juvenile offenses. Superior courts generally function as trial courts, but can also serve as appellate courts to examine disputed cases originally heard in a municipal court.

Generally appeals of disputed cases from lower or "trial" courts rise to the next level, the courts of appeal. These appellate courts re-examine cases based upon legal, not factual, interpretation. There are six district courts of appeal in California helping to relieve the case load of the California supreme court.

The supreme court is the highest court in the state. Its decisions are binding over all other courts. The supreme court hears lower court appeals or may take a case directly from a lower court if it is felt to have constitutional significance. The court consists of a chief justice and six associate justices, serving twelve-year terms. They are appointed by the governor but must be approved by the electorate in the next gubernatorial election. All supreme court and courts of appeal appointments are reviewed and confirmed by a commission on judicial appointments.

The U.S. supreme court will only hear a case from the state court if it involves constitutional issues. The federal court insures that state court rulings and laws passed by the state legislature conform to the U.S. constitution.

In criminal cases, the accused is arrested, arraigned, and either held in custody or released on his or her own recognizance. Criminal cases are categorized as either infractions (minor crimes), misdemeanors (more serious crimes) or felonies (very serious crimes). Plea bargaining is an agreement between the prosecutor and defense attorney to accept a plea of guilty to a lesser crime. Such arrangements ease congestion in the courts, as the accused is convicted without the need of a trial.

Some convicted offenders are allow to serve their prison sentences on probation.

In a criminal case, the district attorney is the prosecuting attorney for the government at the county level. The plaintiff is the entity filing the court action while the defendant is the person being sued or charged with a crime. The defense attorney represents the defendant. In a criminal case, this will often be a public defender when the defendant cannot afford an attorney.

After being arrested, an accused person is entitled to an arraignment before a judge where he or she is formally made aware of the charges and informed of his or her legal rights. At this point the individual may be held in custody, released on bail (as set by the judge) or released on his or her own recognizance.

In civil court, the plaintiff files a case, the defendant is summoned to court, both sides are heard, and a decision, usually involving some payment of damages, is made.

Police officers are employed by a city to uphold justice. Sheriffs work for the county, often functioning as "the police" in unincorporated areas that have no police force. The highway patrol are state peace officers who protect our vast highway system. State police protect state buildings and officials. A marshal is a county peace officer serving our court system, guarding courtrooms, serving court papers and evicting tenants if ordered by the court.

Citizens participate directly in the justice system by serving as witnesses and on juries. In civil and criminal trials, this consists of up to twelve men and women charged with rendering a verdict. A grand jury consists of 19 citizens (23 in Los Angeles). It investigates crimes and government operations and issues a final report to the county board of supervisors.

1. Does the governor appoint all judges?

2. How can the general public remove an unwanted judge?

3. What are the most serious types of crimes?

4. In your opinion, what types of investigations should your grand jury undertake?

5. Can you name at least four types of peace officers?

CITY HALL

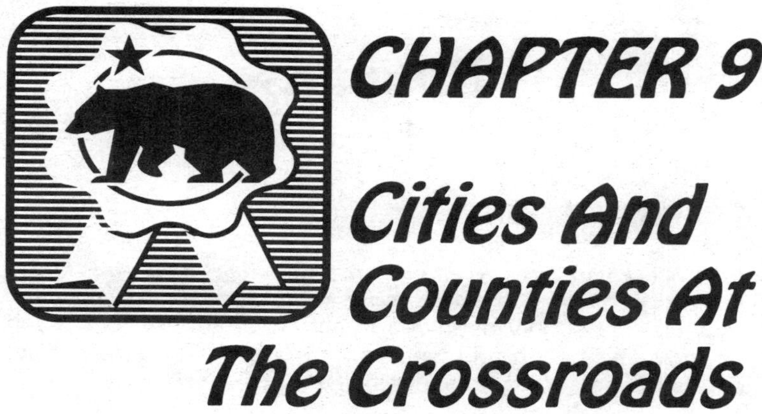

CHAPTER 9

Cities And Counties At The Crossroads

California's local governments are at the crossroads; they are suffering from neglect. There is a lack of political power at the local level. Our cities and counties are designed so that there are no powerful executive leaders; they have no administrative power close to that possessed by the governor of the state or the president of the United States. The mayors have little power to run their cities and power at the county level is too diversified. Let's examine the situation.

Our local governments, which include counties, cities, districts and regions, affect each of us directly on a daily basis. The purpose of this chapter is to familiarize you with: (1) What local government services are available and how they affect all of us; (2) What functions are performed by each segment of our local governments and how to identify them; (3) How each local government unit taxes and what it spends on its operating budget; (4) An overview of how effectively each government unit is performing.

How our local governments are performing:

COUNTIES. . . . . .just barely surviving
CITIES. . . . . .are just getting by
SCHOOL DISTRICTS. . . . . .are in bad shape
OTHER DISTRICTS . . . . are doing well
REGIONS . . . . . . a new solution to local problems?

Counties

TYPES OF COUNTIES

COUNTIES are large geographic areas initially established to bridge the gap between city governments and the state by providing services. The county oversees many important services, such as providing health and welfare, police and fire departments, courts, roads and park services.

The first California Constitution in 1849 provided for the creation of 27 counties and for the election of a board of supervisors in each county. In these early years the county was simply an extension of the legislature and was under its direct control. The Constitutional Revision of 1879 made the functions of counties similar throughout the state, thereby bringing into existence what are known as general law counties. *GENERAL LAW COUNTIES are counties that may establish the number of county officials and their duties, but must have the approval of the state legislature.*

In 1911 the state legislature adopted the Home Rule Amendment which allowed for the creation of charter counties. A *CHARTER (HOME RULE) COUNTY has its own charter (constitution) that allows for more flexibility in collecting revenue-producing taxes, electing and appointing officials and, in general, running and controlling the programs of the county. HOME RULE is the concept that local people are more familiar with, and therefore solve their problems better, than some distant government body.*

COUNTY BOARD OF SUPERVISORS

The COUNTY BOARD OF SUPERVISORS is the county legislature that sets policy and budgets funds. Most boards consist of five members (San Francisco has eleven) who are elected in nonpartisan elections for staggered four-year terms.

COUNTY REVENUES

COUNTY REVENUE is the money that the county receives from all sources. In Los Angeles county, for example, estimated revenue sources, from July 1, 1990 to June 30, 1991, were as follows:

STATE ASSISTANCE (28%)
FEDERAL ASSISTANCE (19%)
PROPERTY TAXES (21%)
SALES TAXES AND OTHER FEES (32%)

State and federal governments contribute 47% toward the budgets of the counties but also require the counties to pay out large sums for the poor through health and welfare programs.

PROPOSITION 13 (PROPERTY TAX LIMITATION)

The fate of our California counties was sealed in 1978 with the passage of Proposition 13 (the Jarvis-Gann property tax initiative). This new law set limits on a major source of revenue for counties; property taxes.

PROPOSITION 13 limits the amount of annual property taxes to a maximum of 1% of the March 1, 1975, market value or selling price of the property, whichever is higher, plus the cumulative increase of 2% each year thereafter.

Before Proposition 13, if the county had a budget shortage, the county would simply increase the property tax rate and pass the costs on to the taxpayer. With real estate values soaring, citizens watched their tax bills soar. Angry homeowners overwhelmingly voted in support of Proposition 13.

As a result of this initiative, county governments saw a massive loss in revenue amounting to billions of dollars each year. The state had to pour large amounts of money into the counties, cities, school districts, etc., just to cover some of the loss. Thus, a great deal of the policy making function has moved to the legislature in Sacramento.

OTHER COUNTY OFFICIALS

1. Chief Administrative Officer
2. District Attorney and Public Defender
3. Assessor and Treasurer
4. Sheriff

THE NUMBER OF COUNTIES HAS GROWN TO 58

The original boundaries of the 27 counties have been split and redrawn over the years to the present 58 counties. The counties in California vary widely as to size, political makeup and geography.

FUNCTIONS OF THE COUNTY

Whether under the laws of the state in general law counties, or the guidelines of the charter in home rule counties, each county has certain duties and responsibilities that must be performed. Many of these functions are delegated to the board of supervisors, who are responsible for their implementation and continuous supervision. Some of the more important county functions are:

1. **Education** - county superintendent of schools is responsible for the overall administration and distribution of funds to schools (K-community college).
2. **Law enforcement and protection of property** - the county sheriff is responsible for the areas in the county outside of larger cities, which generally have their own police departments.
3. **Local Agency Formation Commission (LAFCO)** - a county board of supervisor's-created body whose function is to determine the boundaries of any proposed incorporated city within that county's area.
4. **Bridges and highways** - It is a county's responsibility to maintain the roads that lead into the main highways.
5. **Recreation** - each county maintains county parks.
6. **General government** - the collection of taxes by the county tax collector. From these taxes the county derives its budget.

Hispanic Council District

THE POWERFUL L. A. COUNTY BOARD OF SUPERVISORS

The ***REDISTRICTING BY LAWSUIT*** judgment created a Hispanic county district. Supervisor Gloria Molina of the newly created 1st District is the first Hispanic member to serve in over 115 years. Her presence, plus another newly elected member, will greatly change the make-up of the five-member Los Angeles County Board of Supervisors, which has traditionally been dominated by white, conservative male Republicans.

COUNTIES LACK EXECUTIVE MANAGEMENT

One of the biggest shortcomings of county government is the inability of the public to key-in on one individual as being responsible for the condition of county government. Each county has at least five supervisors acting as its executive authority, making it impossible to single out any individual as being responsible for inaction. The state may have a twelve person plural executive, but the responsibility rests with the governor. Some counties have experimented with a chief administrative officer, appointed by the board of supervisors to carry out its programs. Even with this position, most citizens are still lost when it comes to understanding with whom the responsibility of county government lies.

COUNTY EXPENDITURES

COUNTY EXPENDITURES are the monies that are spent by a county to operate. The money is disbursed in the form of a budget. The average budget that the board of supervisors in each county is responsible for is broken down as follows:

WELFARE AND SOCIAL SERVICES	26.5%
COUNTY HOSPITALS, PUBLIC HEALTH	23.7%
SHERIFF, JAIL, COURTS	20.7%
PUBLIC WORKS — ROADS	10.0%
GENERAL GOVERNMENT OFFICES	3.7%
FIRE PROTECTION	3.6%
RECREATION AND CULTURAL	2.8%
COMMUNITY DEVELOPMENT HOUSING	2.5%
INSURANCE AND RESERVES	6.5%
	100%

Note that welfare, health, law enforcement and roads account for almost the entire county budget, leaving little available for other needed services.

Cities

A CITY IS CREATED BY INCORPORATING

In 1883, the California state legislature adopted the Municipal Corporations Act, which classified cities according to population and laid the groundwork for future incorporation of cities. ***INCORPORATION** is the process of legally forming a public corporation.* When referring to an incorporated area, one is talking about a city. An ***UNINCORPORATED AREA** is a part of a county that is not an independently recognized city.*

To incorporate, a community must petition the county board of supervisors. The Local Agency Formation Commission (LAFCO) then holds hearings at which time the boundaries of the proposed city are set. A ***LOCAL AGENCY FORMATION COMMISSION** is the group that defines the exact boundary lines of cities and counties.* After approval by the LAFCO, an election is then called.

Previous to Proposition 13, homeowners in cities found themselves taxed twice; paying property taxes to both the county and city. Since the passage of Proposition 13, the city property tax is subtracted from the county property tax. Because of this, there is no longer any reason, for most areas, not to incorporate.

GENERAL LAW CITIES

All newly incorporated cities must begin their existence as general law cities. In a *GENERAL LAW CITY government functions are administered by a five-member city council, elected for four-year terms.* A city clerk and treasurer are also elected for four-year terms. Other officials are appointed by the council. The mayor is chosen from the council. Some cities have a city manager or chief administrator, appointed by the city council to carry out its programs. This person holds office only as long as the council desires.

CHARTER (HOME RULE) CITIES

After a city becomes a general law city, it may frame a charter of its own, much like a county, and become a charter city. A *CHARTER CITY frames its own charter, enabling its citizens to better deal with current problems.* Most cities with populations over 100,000 in California are charter cities.

The main advantage of a charter city is its increased power with regard to local control and government function. A charter city can exceed the tax rate that is imposed on general law cities. It can perform any municipal functions that do not violate state or national laws. Most importantly, it allows the people of the city to adjust their government to meet any special needs.

MAYOR-COUNCIL vs. COUNCIL-MANAGER

In a mayor-council type of city government, a *MAYOR is the chief executive officer of the city,* and the *CITY COUNCIL is usually a five to fifteen member nonpartisan board that is elected to handle the executive business of the city.* A *STRONG MAYOR SYSTEM usually allows the mayor some veto power over the council and power to appoint and remove certain city officials.* The best example of a strong mayor system in California is the city of San Francisco. A *WEAK MAYOR SYSTEM is one in which the office of mayor is more a ceremonial position, with the mayor being selected from among the city council members.*

In a council-manager form of city government, the people elect a city council and a mayor. This is the most popular form of city government in California. The duties of the mayor are mostly ceremonial in nature. The council appoints a city manager to conduct the business of the city. A *CITY MANAGER is a professional manager who implements the city council's programs.* Over the years the shift has been from a engineering background for a city manager toward a business background.

OTHER CITY ADMINISTRATORS

1. City attorneys (prosecutors/public defenders)
2. City clerk
3. Police chief
4. Fire chief
5. Fiscal officials
6. Planning and community development officials
7. Public works officials
8. Recreation, parks and community services officials
9. Librarians

HOW CITIES ACQUIRE AND SPEND THEIR MONEY

A city acquires most of its funds from fees and activities that occur or are generated within the city. The following is an example of where city revenue might come from:

City Revenue

Sales, Business Utility and Hotel Taxes	49.5%
Property Taxes	12.1%
Licenses and Permits	7.1%
Fines and Violations	5.5%

COUNTIES BILL CITIES FOR SERVICES

Proposition 13 has basically fixed tax rates. The decreasing amount of funds at the county level has given the state legislature increased power over the counties. This has forced the counties to increase sales taxes.

In 1990 the state legislature allowed our under-funded counties to charge the cities within their county a "prisoner booking fee" and "property tax collection fee." This greatly concerns our California cities because they see this as the first in a series of steps that could mandate programs in the county for which the cities would be charged.

The city government provides the following services:

1. **Protective services** - The highest percentage of funds is spent on these, including law enforcement, fire protection and civil defense.
2. **Recreation, health, education** - This includes parks and playgrounds. Health services are often in conjunction with county programs. Schools are run and maintained through school districts.
3. **Public works -** Improvement and maintenance of city streets, off-street parking, collection of trash and sanitation.
4. **General government** - Most cities utilize the county tax facilities to collect tax money.

Districts

DISTRICT FUNCTIONS

DISTRICTS are geographic units designated for a specific governmental purpose, usually to provide a public service, such as mosquito abatement, flood control and education.

Districts can co-exist with a city or county but often they do not. There are about 6,000 districts in California, of which at least 1,000 are school districts.

CREATION OF A DISTRICT

The establishment and organization of districts is provided for by state law. In order to form a district, a petition must be signed by the voters living within the boundaries of the proposed district. This petition is presented to the board of supervisors. A majority vote is needed by the board, or in some cases the electorate, to establish a district.

SCHOOL DISTRICTS

The largest category of districts is the school districts. There are over 1,000 school districts in California. Every segment of California is divided into school districts. School districts include: elementary, high school, unified (K-12 grades), union (high school district that encompasses several elementary districts), and community college.

Each school district has a board of education. The board of education generally consists of five members chosen in a nonpartisan election held within each district. The board has the responsibility of hiring principals, teachers and all support staff for the district. It also adopts the school budget and determines the curriculum.

Each board is accountable to the state board of education, the ten member board appointed by the governor and administered by the state superintendent of public instruction. Each community college board has more individual power to govern its own district. It is overseen by the state board of governors of the community colleges.

WATER DISTRICTS

The Metropolitan (MWD) Water District was organized to provide Southern California with water to supplement its dwindling water supply.

Running along the Pacific Ocean from Oxnard to the Mexican border and inland for 70 miles, the MWD extends into six counties: San Diego, San Bernardino, Riverside, Orange, Los Angeles and Ventura. The MWD supplies about half of the water used within its service area and is expected to handle nearly all of the anticipated increases in the future. Of course, the amount of water supplied will depend on the amount of snow that falls in the northern Sierra mountains.

Electric Cars ... Starting In 1998

California has mandated that electric cars must be mass-produced beginning in 1998. Under the adapted plan, 2% (about 20,000 to 25, 000) of the new cars sold in California each year must be emission-free. The volume increases to 5% in 2001 and to 10% in 2003. Companies violating the standard could lose their certification to sell cars in California.

As the deadline approaches, the Big Three auto makers have been putting increasing pressure on California to grant delays. They claim that it is impossible for them to meet this deadline. The Air Resources Board (ARB) claims that there should be no trouble in meeting the deadline. Watch this issue as 1998 approaches.

Regional Governance

TREND FROM COUNTY TO REGIONAL DISTRICTS

The dramatic growth of Los Angeles, Ventura, Orange, Riverside and San Bernardino counties has created a mostly urban area where the boundaries of counties and cities are so close together that they are hard to distinguish.

A *REGION is a large geographic unit that can include many cities and counties and cover a large portion of a state.* Their common problems have led to the idea of regional governance.

REGIONAL GOVERNANCE is the process of regional planning and policy making with the help of cities, counties and businesses within the region. Water shortages, air pollution and transportation are just some of the issues which cross city or county lines and might be handled more efficiently at the regional level. When counties or cities are overwhelmed by a problem and underwhelmed by the resources needed to handle it, a regional approach seems to be the best answer.

Regional financing is the new way to solve regional problems. Los Angeles county is now collecting an additional 1/2 cent sales tax to help solve transportation problems by linking together transit lines from many cities within the county. The Metropolitan Water District helps furnish most of the water for Southern California and bills according to usage. This trend will continue with regard to our air quality and waste management.

COUNCILS OF GOVERNMENT

*A **COUNCIL OF GOVERNMENT (COG's)** is an association of city and county government officials, within a given region, whose purpose is to find solutions to common problems.* These COG's help solve common area problems quickly and cooperatively while maintaining the home rule style of government.

The Southern California Association of Government, known as SCAG, and the Association of Bay Area Government, known as ABAG, are California's two major COG's.

ABAG has been successful in making regional plans for such important matters as transportation, refuse disposal, recreational facilities and shoreline development. The SCAG is the largest COG in the United States, serving over 13 million people in a 38,000 square mile area. SCAG has been successful in coordinating the planned connection between the Southern California Rapid Transit District (SCRTD) and the Orange County Transit District (OCTD) transit lines.

Most of California's regional problems are not being financed or solved by the federal or state government. Clean air and pollution standards by the Air Quality Management District (AQMD) have been made strict to reduce air pollution for the region. Federal standards, although well meaning, do not take into account Southern California's unique air pollution problems. So basically the federal government has complicated matters rather than offered viable solutions. Frankly, the state and federal governments have given Southern California mandates regarding air pollution but have not given the area the funds with which to accomplish these mandates. ***MANDATES** are the requirements for programs implemented by the state or federal government.*

Our California city and county governments face great challenges for the future. Greater demands are being placed on them than ever before, but local government lacks the definitive political clout necessary to effectively administer these services.

Counties are large geographical areas that bridge the gap between cities and the state by providing services at the local level. The California constitution created the original 27 counties. There are now 58. The original counties were considered general law counties, and functioned only under the close supervision of the state legislature. Later, under the Home Rule Amendment of 1911, counties were permitted to designate themselves as charter (or home rule) counties permitting more autonomy to set policy and collect taxes.

County government is administered by a County Board of Supervisors, usually five members elected to four-year terms. They decide public policy, budget funds and make various local appointments. County governments are primarily responsible for several important public functions: Education, law enforcement, Local Agency Formation Commission (LAFCO), maintenance of bridges and highways, recreation, and taxes.

County revenue also comes from the state (28%), the federal government (19%), property taxes (21%), sales taxes and other fees (32%). These state and federal contributions are not without strings attached, and most of the money they give the counties is passed on directly to the public as health and welfare programs.

In 1978 Proposition 13 passed, limiting the amount of property taxes that could be collected by the county. Local governments saw a loss in revenue and the state had to fill the void, pouring millions of dollars into the counties to keep their schools, law enforcement, recreation and other necessary programs operating. But with each dollar came more state control.

Counties spend most of their budgets on welfare and social services (26.5%), county hospitals and public health (23.7%), as well as the county sheriff, jails and courts (20.7%). Very little is left for other needed areas such as government offices (3.7%), fire protection (3.6%), recreation and culture (2.8%), community development and housing (2.5%), insurance and cash reserves (6.5%).

Cities are created by becoming incorporated; a process that is similar to forming a business corporation. They are formed from unincorporated areas of the county or split from other cities with the proper voters' approval. All cities start as general law cities but most become charter (home rule) cities when their population grows.

In the mayor-council form of city the mayor and council direct the different agencies that run the city. These cities are governed by a nonpartisan elected board of 5 to 15 members called a city council and a mayor who is selected to lead this group. Either the mayor is elected by the city council or is elected separately by the voters. If the mayor comes from a weak mayor system the duties are mostly ceremonial. In a strong mayor system the mayor can make appointments and remove certain city officials.

In a council-manager form of city, which is the most common in California, the city is run by a professional city manager.

Although cities vary greatly, most cities collect their money from these sources: Sales taxes and hotel taxes, real property taxes, Cigarette taxes, development and other fees. Cities spend their money mostly on: 1) police and fire protection; 2) health, recreation and education; 3) public works, off-street parking and sanitation; 4) city personnel and elections.

There are about 6,000 districts in California. Districts are geographical units designed for a specific governmental purpose, such as flood control, mosquito abatement or for schools. Their are more than 1,000 school districts (K-12 and community college). Perhaps one of the best known districts is the Metropolitan Water District.

Regional governance may take the place of a local government on certain issues in the future because many of California's problems cross over city and county lines.

1. What made the formation of California cities so popular?
2. What are the effects on the state caused by such diverse cultural and ethnic backgrounds?
3. What are the differences between California cities using weak and strong mayoral systems?
4. What are the pros and cons of an at large election?
5. What are the strong and weak points of (county, city, district and regional) governmental units in California?

CHAPTER 10 Our State Budget Crisis

CALIFORNIA'S STATE BUDGET CRISIS

The California state budget crisis is directly related to our constantly increasing population growth. Our population has grown so fast over the last two decades and is still growing so fast that the state's resources cannot keep up with all the added demands. California's highways are congested, schools are overcrowded, the air is polluted, more landfills are closing and more people than ever are on welfare and county health care: The system cannot keep up.

Remember, it is estimated that California's population will increase by 6 million between 1990 and the year 2000. Further, it is projected that our population will increase another 6 million between 2000 and 2010. No matter how one looks at our state's growth pattern, it is constantly growing larger.

Some may say that all we need to correct our budget crisis are higher taxes and new laws. I'm afraid not! Our taxes are at an all-time high and if they are increased even more, businesses will leave the state, taking with them needed jobs. Californians are already among the highest taxed people in the United States. The solution is to operate our state government more like a business. With some good leadership from state and local politicians, the problems facing California can be addressed. The state has run out of the simple answer—more taxes. What is left are hard political choices about where to cut spending to get the most out of budget dollars.

California Is Growing Older and Younger

California's population is growing both older and younger at the same time. Our retired population is booming while the number of children is growing at an unprecedented rate. The working group in the middle that pays most of the taxes is declining. To illustrate this point, California can be divided into three groups:

1. **EARNERS** (Age 18 to 64. Working population)
2. **SPENDERS** (65 and older. Social security and pensioners)
3. **USERS** (Mostly under 18. They receive public services: education, child care and welfare)

"Earners" are declining in percentage terms. Parents of the baby boomers are retiring and soon the baby boomers themselves will start leaving the work force.

"Spenders" are retirees living on social security who are positive contributors to the economy because they spend money and pay more than their fair share in state sales taxes.

The **"users"** group are younger and use California's public service tax dollars in the form of education, child care and welfare. The huge growth within this group is largely due to the increasing immigrant population.

The end effect of these demographic changes is that they drive up state and local government spending, while at the same time reducing the revenue generated by state income taxes and sales taxes. This is the cause of the California budget crisis.

Quinn, Tony (demographics-expert), Vice President of Braun Ketchum, a public relations firm based in Sacramento

THE RECESSION OF 1990-1993

The state went into a severe financial crisis starting in 1990 with a huge shortfall in state taxes caused by the recession. State spending for most programs was reduced or slashed. Taxes were increased on personal and business income, renters faced the loss of credits and everyone had to pay a higher sales tax on more items. But this was not the end. Through 1998 there will be more and deeper cuts in state programs. Remember: the days of easy answers are over for California—only hard choices lie ahead.

The California State Budget

The *STATE BUDGET is the state government's financial plan for spending and taxing that is proposed by the governor and passed by the legislature for each fiscal year.*

Federal, state and county governments use a fiscal year instead of a calendar year. The *GOVERNMENTAL FISCAL YEAR is a 365 day year that starts on July 1st and ends on June 30th.* For example, if the governor, mayor or a school board member refers to the 1995-1996 fiscal year, they are referring to the year from July 1, 1995 to June 30, 1996.

No deficits are allowed in state budgets. A *DEFICIT occurs when current money, collected in taxes, is not enough to pay for the agreed upon expenses.*

THE BUDGET PROCESS

The budget process covers an 18—month period and is complicated. The budget phases (lasting six months each) are:

1. The budget construction phase—"what do you want" stage.

2. The department of finance refinement phase— "let's be realistic" stage.

3. The legislative debate and vote phase—"they are only getting what we give them" stage.

Each January, after the governor's State of the State Address, the budget is submitted to the legislature. The legislature, after debating it at length and passing it with the required two-thirds vote of both houses, submits the approved budget to the governor. The submission date to the governor is June 15th. The legislature has often failed to meet this deadline.

Remember: the governor has line item veto power. The *LINE ITEM VETO means the governor can eliminate or reduce any budget item he or she does not like.* The budget then goes back to the legislature, which has the constitutional power to override the governor's veto with a two-thirds vote in each house. They seldom succeed.

SPENDING LIMITATIONS

Spending limitation propositions limited the amount of tax revenues that state and local governments could spend in any given year. The dollar amount of this limitation could only be adjusted upward by the annual percentage rate of inflation plus the annual percentage rate of population growth. But that was before our demographic shift showed that the number of children increased, the number of welfare recipients increased, the number of people who needed county health services increased and the number of cars on the highways increased.

Proposition 98 established minimum levels of spending for schools and community colleges. Proposition 99 increased cigarette and tobacco taxes, but earmarked these funds for specific anti-smoking programs.

CALIFORNIA'S BUDGET PROBLEMS

The crisis of the 1990's and beyond is: How will California handle its growth problems in a state where the residents are already among the most taxed in the country? There are only difficult answers when seeking ways to reduce the budget. Reasonable solutions to our growth problems must be prioritized. The budget can then be tightened by searching for new, practical answers. The budget problems created by our extensive population growth over the past decades are here. How will we deal with all these problems at once?

Types of State Taxes

THE FOUR MAIN TAXES

In order to understand California's basic tax structure, it is best to look at the four main sources of state taxes. Who pays and what the rate paid are political questions. The state's taxing policy, which is implemented by our governor and legislature, constantly changes over time.

State Taxes 1994 — 95
Where State Taxes Come From:

	Source	Share
#1	Personal Income Taxes	43.8%
#2	State Sales Tax	34.9%
#3	Bank & Corporation Income Taxes	11.6%
#4	Insurance Tax	3.0%
#5	Tobacco Tax	.4%
#6	Estate Tax	1.2%
#7	Alcohol Tax	.7%
#8	Federal Fund Recoveries	.8%
#9	Miscellaneous Minor Taxes	3.6%

#1—State Personal Income Taxes

The *STATE FRANCHISE TAX BOARD is the California state agency that collects state income taxes from individuals and corporations.* The state personal income tax is the single largest source of taxes in California. Currently the state income tax rate goes up to 11% for those in the highest bracket. But remember, federal income taxes, which have a top rate of 39.6%, must be paid in addition to the state income taxes. Some other states, such as Nevada, Florida and Washington, do not even charge their citizens any personal income tax. This is another reason why some of our more affluent residents are tempted to leave California.

State income taxes are indexed. *INDEXING is the periodic adjustment of income tax brackets to eliminate the effects of inflation.*

This means that if the inflation rate is 3% for the year, the tax bracket will also go up by 3% to compensate for the difference. The taxpayer, although making more money, may still remain in the same tax bracket. This makes our legislators more accountable to us because income tax revenues do not automatically increase due to increased inflation.

#2—State Sales Taxes

The *STATE BOARD OF EQUALIZATION is the California state agency that collects state sales taxes from businesses that, in turn, collect taxes from the consumer at the point of purchase.* Wholesalers do not pay sales tax because they are not the ultimate consumer. The current sales tax rate is 7 1/2%, but this rate can be increased on an individual county basis, if approved by the voters, by up to 3/4 of a percent for transportation or other uses.

#3—Bank & Corporation Income Taxes

The state also collects income taxes on corporations, whose shares of stock are mostly owned by individuals, and the pension plans of most unions or businesses. With personal (43.8%) and corporate income taxes (11.6%), California receives 55.4% of its revenue from income taxes.

#4—Other Miscellaneous Taxes

All the remaining types of taxes combined add up to just under 10%. They are taxes on gas and diesel fuel, insurance, tobacco, alcohol, inheritance, horse racing and other minor state taxes. There are a large number of these smaller types of taxes that affect almost every aspect of our lives.

TAXES AFFECTS THE POOR AND THE WEALTHY

Taxes do not affect all people the same way. Certain taxes affect the poor more than the wealthy and certain taxes hardly affect the poor but definitely hurt the wealthy. The goal should be a tax policy that requires very little from the poor and more (but not too much) from the wealthy. Of course, the same policy would collect most of the taxes from the middle group referred to as "average" Californians.

A *REGRESSIVE TAX is a tax that is larger, as a percentage, for lower income people.* A good example of a regressive tax is the California state sales tax. This tax takes up a larger portion of the lower income individual's personal budget because almost all of his or her income is used to buy items subject to this tax. It has a big impact on people who have the least amount of money. If the same tax rate is paid by all, it is regressive.

A *PROGRESSIVE TAX is a tax that increases, percentage-wise, as the wealth of the taxpayer increases.* The best example of a progressive tax is the California state income tax on individuals and businesses. Poor people may not pay any income taxes, middle income Californians pay a large amount and the wealthy pay the most, on an individual basis. This tax affects the rich the most because they are in the highest tax bracket and therefore pay the most money.

SIN TAXES are the taxes paid for the purchase and consumption of alcoholic beverages and tobacco products. These taxes have increased dramatically in recent years. The tax is not only applied to hard liquors but also to wines and beers.

TAXES WILL REMAIN HIGH

California's taxes will remain high in the foreseeable future because of the many problems created by our continuous population growth. Most of the badly needed solutions will require funds the state does not possess. The challenge to the political leadership is: How will it decide, among competing alternatives, which programs will receive the most money?

Spending: Where Taxes Go

THE FIVE LARGEST EXPENDITURES

The five largest expenditures represent 86.3% of the state's budget. In descending order of cost, they are: #1 Schools and Community Colleges; #2 Health and Welfare; #3 Higher Education; #4 Prisons and the Youth Authority; and #5 Courts, Legislation and General Government. There is little money remaining in the budget for newer, more innovative programs after these big costly programs are funded.

#1 COST—Education K-12 and Community Colleges

More money is spent on educating our students from kindergarten through high school and supporting community college students than on any other state function. Education represents over one-third of the state budget. Each school or college district is technically owned by the state but governed, controlled and administered by a local board that is elected by the voters. *LOCAL CONTROL means that the administrators and teachers are hired by the local board of education to administer and teach the subjects approved by the board.*

The state provides 85% of all the educational costs to each district. About 12% of the money for schools and community colleges comes from the local governments that collect funds in the form of real estate property taxes. In addition, the state lottery generates about 3% of the funds.

It costs over $ 3,000 a year, per student, to educate a child in the K-12 public school system. Further, most community college students do not realize that it costs over $3,200 annually to educate a full-time student. Even though community colleges charge students about $150 a year for tuition and fees, they are still getting one of the best educational bargains anywhere in the United States.

#2 COST—Health and Welfare

Health Services: Public health care has been constantly declining because of the relentless population increases over the last two decades. Providing health services to Californians who do not have health insurance is nearly impossible under the current system. The number of people who want free health care keeps rising. The cost of all health care is increasing at such a fast pace that even a good state health program would not be able to keep up under current legislation.

The cost of private health care in the United States, which is the best in the world, is rising about 15% annually. If the state cannot find a way to contain the cost of the private health care system, how can there ever be a good public system? This cannot be achieved without major legislative changes and citizens' commitment. Almost no one, though, wants to give up the current private health insurance programs, so an acceptable solution would have to integrate a public system with the current private system.

Welfare: California has 12% of the U.S. population but must support 16% of the nation's welfare recipients. Unfortunately, each year welfare continues to take up a larger and larger portion of the state budget.

Governor Pete Wilson has said, "Welfare was designed as temporary assistance...California can no longer afford to pay people not to work." The governor's idea is to push people off welfare by reducing their grants and giving them incentives to go to work. Hopefully this will break the cycle of poverty that welfare dependency has created.

Wilson's Reforms

Governor Wilson says "The Welfare System is chasing jobs out of the state." He has also warned that the financing of education is being threatened by runaway welfare costs. His welfare reforms now in the courts include:

1. Some family benefits will be cut by 25%.
2. Another 15% will be cut after six months for families with an able-bodied adult in the house.
3. Teenage mothers would have a $50 per month incentive to stay in school and a $50 a month penalty if they drop out.
4. Families moving into California from out of state would be eligible (for their first year here) only for the same AFDC benefits they would have received in their former state.

#3 COST—Higher Education

University students are suffering huge fee increases. The state budget crisis of 1991 had the effect of forcing students on University of California campuses to pay more for tuition. Students in the California State University system had a "whopping" increase of 40%. Higher education in California may still be a bargain, but the good old days are gone.

State Spending 1994-95

Spending Of Tax Money:

#1	Education (K-12, Community Colleges)	39.1%
#2	Health and Welfare	34.2%
#3	Higher Education	9.2%
#4	Prisons, Youth Authority	9.1%
#5	Courts/Legislature/General Government	3.8%
#6	Natural Resources	1.7%
#7	Tax Relief (Homeowners & Seniors)	1.2%
#8	State & Consumer Services	.9%
#9	Business, Transportation & Housing	.6%
#10	Environmental Protection Agency	.2%

#4 COST—Prisons, Youth Authority

There are over 100,000 men and women in California prisons, more than any other state and four times greater than only a decade ago. It is projected there will be over 200,000 prisoners by the year 2000—3-strikes will make this figure even higher.

The public's fear of crime, which is fed by the news media, demands that politicians be tough on criminals. The problem is that it costs over $20,000 a year to house a prisoner. In many respects it would benefit us to come up with alternatives to prisons for non-violent offenses, such as individual abuse of drugs or alcohol. If the state could reduce the annual $3.8 billion budget by one billion, just think of the possibilities.

5 COST—Courts, Legislation and Government

California's court system costs have been increasing and will have large further increases since the passage of the 3-strikes legislation. The costs of running the legislature are up some because the legislators are under term limitations and therefore require more help. Of course the cost of running the government in Sacramento is large and will continue to be so.

MOST SPENDING IS EARMARKED

Most state government spending is earmarked for special purposes. ***EARMARKED FUNDS*** *have been committed and budgeted ahead of time to accomplish a certain purpose.* Earmarked funds for gas taxes approved a decade ago must be used to build highways, even though the state now needs to use the funds elsewhere. As public needs change, our government becomes handcuffed because it can't spend earmarked funds.

Bonds Mean Debt

When the state of California needs to borrow money, the amount is too large to be obtained from a lending institution. The state must sell bonds to the general public in order to raise funds. A ***BOND*** *is a debt, a loan in increments of $1,000, made to the state of California, which will be repaid by the state to the owner of the bond on a certain date, usually in 20 years.* In effect, this is an installment credit program to purchase buildings or finance construction projects. Voters must approve each bond issue. There are two types of bonds.

A ***GENERAL OBLIGATION BOND*** *is secured by everything the state owns.* It is used when the project the bond is funding will not earn money. The other type of bond is a revenue bond. A ***REVENUE BOND*** *is backed up only by the revenue generated by that project or taxing district.* The state uses revenue bonds to finance dams, canals, bridges and other projects that can generate income. Buyers of these bonds rely on credit rating agencies to analyze the credit worthiness of the issue.

Credit Agency Lowers Our Ranking

Standard and Poor's, a major Wall Street credit agency, has steadily downgraded California's credit rating. They are alarmed by our "chronic deficit operations" and the inability to overcome budget problems. Bond ratings are used by investment firms to calculate interest rates that the state of California must pay to borrowers.

But there is a danger of approving too many bonds because the bonds, including interest, must eventually be paid off just as one would be required to do with personal credit card loans. Bonds represent spending. The difference is that the state pays off the expenditure over a long period of time. Our children will end up paying for these bonds.

Business Climate

Governor Wilson has said, with good reason, "California's business climate is in desperate need of improvement." Employers leave this state fleeing both the present burden of taxation and the ever-present threat that autopilot spending will make the tax burden even heavier. California will lose more jobs unless we work to provide fundamental budget reform and control of state spending.

A healthy business climate creates and keeps jobs. Until recently, California citizens never thought business would leave the state. In the 1990's we now understand that companies will leave if costly taxes or needless regulations are put in their way.

KEEPING BUSINESS IN CALIFORNIA

Governor Wilson created a 17-member, bipartisan team of business and labor leaders (Council on California Competitiveness) to find ways to attract businesses to California and keep companies from leaving. According to the leader of the council, Peter V. Ueberroth: "We are frightened about the state's future, California must create about 300,000 new jobs each year to generate enough taxes to pay for such government services as health, welfare and schools for our 600,000 new annual residents."

WHAT BUSINESSES SHOULD WE ATTRACT!

California's economy has always been growing by attracting new and emerging firms and industries. Remember, California's economic strengths are:

Pacific Rim trade
Technology-oriented manufacturing
Entertainment and tourism
Engineering, design, finance, management and software.

California's economy has developed into a high-value-added environment with high wages and high cost locations. We attract innovative companies that are on the cutting edge. These types of companies come here because of the state's strengths. These are the types of companies that we should be encouraging to do business in California.

Some companies are leaving California. These firms are generally in maturing industries in need of lower tax and wage bases. There may be little that can be done to keep them in California, but the state should attempt to do so.

California's continued growth depends on attracting the next generation of growth firms. We should be asking fast growing companies why they located here instead of asking firms why they are leaving. This focus on growth, always looking ahead, is the right direction for the state's economy.

California's state budget is in a crisis. There is not enough money coming in to cover the cost of all the services the state provides. This problem is worsening due to relentless population growth. Every decade we add another six million people to drain already limited resources. Raising taxes is not the answer. Higher taxes only drive businesses away to other states or countries where they can operate less expensively. If businesses leave, so do jobs and tax money, damaging the economy even more. There are no simple answers anymore. The future of California will depend on careful planning and intelligent leadership, so the state can provide for the growing population without bankrupting itself.

Our problems are the result of the population distribution between three economic groups; "earners," "spenders," and "users." "Earners" are the working population, ages 18 to 64. They pay most of the taxes and really fuel the economy. Unfortunately this group is declining as a percentage of the population. We are losing our core working group and seeing an increase in the younger and older populations. The younger group contributes far less to the economy. The older group, or "spenders," are retirees living on social security. They are good for the economy because they spend money and pay more in state sales taxes. The biggest economic drain on the state is the "users" group, made up of children.

The state budget is the government's plan for spending and taxing for the next fiscal year. The fiscal year begins July 1st and ends June 30th. A deficit occurs when the tax money collected is not enough to cover the agreed upon expenses. California, by law, must have a balanced budget—No deficit.

Money collected from the California personal income tax is the state's primary source of revenue. People in the highest brackets pay 11% of their income to the State Franchise Tax Board. The second largest sources of revenue is the state sales tax, charged by the State Board of Equalization, on retail purchases. The current state sales tax rate is 7 1/2%, although many counties add their own sales tax on top of this for local uses. Our third largest taxing source is the income tax collected from banks and corporations. This accounts for 8.8% of the state's funding. The vehicle and licensing fees collected by the Department of Motor Vehicles are the fourth source.

The state sales tax is a "regressive tax." The same rate of tax is paid by rich and poor alike, but the sales tax hits poor people harder because they spend most of their money on items subject to this tax. A "progressive tax" is one that increases percentage-wise as the wealth of the taxpayer increases. The state income tax is a good example. People with higher incomes are required to pay a higher tax rate.

Education is the prime expenditure of the California state budget. The fiscal budget for K-12 and community colleges is 39.1% of the budget. Health and welfare is the state's number two expense at 34.2%. Higher education, the University of

California and Cal-State systems, has a cost of 9.2%. Prisons take up 9.1% of the budget. An effort is being made to turn these huge numbers around. Community colleges and state universities are raising fees and tuition—The budget crisis is killing the concept of an affordable college education.

When funds are committed in advance for a specific program, they are said to be "earmarked." Lottery money being used for public schools, or gas taxes to build highways, are good examples. The problem with earmarked funds is they deprive our government officials of discretion as priorities change.

When the state needs to borrow large amounts of money it issues "bonds." Bonds are a form of debt. The state borrows from the general public in increments of $1,000. These bonds are paid off later with interest. General obligation bonds are secured by all California assets for any purpose. Revenue bonds are backed up only by the particular project for which the bond was issued. They finance public works projects designed to pay for themselves, such as toll roads and hydroelectric dams. Traditionally California bonds have been considered a solid investment, although in recent years, due largely to our ongoing budget crisis, a major Wall Street credit agency has down-graded California state bonds. Until our credit rating improves, the state will be forced to pay a higher rate of interest to compensate bondholders.

1. What types of taxes generate the most income?

2. List the main expenditures of the state. What percentage of the budget is available for new programs?

3. Is the state sales tax or the state income tax more regressive or progressive in nature?

4. Of what significance is the fact that the state's population is growing older and younger at the same time?

5. When voters approve bonds, who will pay it off?

Index

California State & Local Government In Crisis

Walt Huber